LUCKY JACK (1894-2000)

Buried alive...twice. Survived a WW1 POW camp. Drove through London with no brakes and lived to tell these tales!

S. BAVEY

josephtailor

Photos to accompany this book can be viewed at
https://suelbavey.wordpress.com/lucky-jack-
photo-gallery/

PART I
HUMBLE BEGINNINGS

CHAPTER 1
HELLO, PLEASED TO MEET YOU,
WELCOME TO MY WORLD!

My name is Henry John Rogers, but I'm known to most people as Jack.

I was born at the very end of the nineteenth century, on 21st March 1894, in a room above my father's boot repair shop, in Hammersmith, London.

Most of my nine siblings (I was the second eldest) were born in the same room. Of course, I had no idea then that my life would be full of adventure, that I would live through two world wars - serving in one - and that I would even be a (relatively) famous newspaper columnist!

My life has been full of love, laughter, music and comedy, all 106 years - yes, I've managed to live in three different centuries! I've known hunger, fear, and loss, but I've also had the privilege of a happy marriage, and wonderful friends.

I hope you enjoy my story.

My father, Harry Rogers, owned his own shoe repair business, and, although we were poor, we did have a roof over our heads. I had seven sisters and two brothers, so my mother, Clara, had her hands full!

We moved from the apartment above the shop to a house on Goldhawk Road in 1906 where my brother, Frederick William (Freddie) was born in 1907. Six and a half years later my mother gave birth to a little girl called Clara Winifred, named after my dear mother. My mother was almost fifty by then and little Clara was very tiny, like a little dolly. She was beautiful and I remember my mother nursing her by the fire. Sadly, my baby sister only lived for a month. I remember that they put her tiny white coffin under the hearse driver's seat and then she was buried along with an adult for a small cost. That was how very young children of poor people were buried at the time.

From left to right: Beattie, Nell, Jack, Will Price (later
May's husband, May, Rose. Middle: parents Harry and
Clara. Front: Minnie, Freddie, Florrie.

PART II
CHILDHOOD DAYS

CHAPTER 3

A SPECIAL SMILE FROM QUEEN VICTORIA

hen I was only three years old, I was lucky enough to be in the crowds for Queen Victoria's Diamond Jubilee on June 22nd, 1897.

There were thousands of people thronging the streets and I couldn't understand what was happening. We had walked for six hours from Hammersmith up to the Strand, on a scorchingly hot day. I was wearing a plum-coloured velvet suit, despite the temperature, and felt like the bees' knees. We waited for hours, but there was a feeling of excitement in the air and it kept us going. It was well worth the effort to see the 'old lady', as we called her, in her horse-drawn carriage and carrying a white parasol. My father was a tall man and so I had a great view from up on his shoulders and was clearly visible to Her Majesty from among the five thousand people gathered, or so I am convinced to this day. As the carriage slowly approached the place where we were standing, Her Majesty turned towards us and I caught her eye. She smiled at me and nodded! I'm sure she wasn't just aiming her smile and nod

at me but at such a tender age, it certainly felt like. I was
sure that my dapper attire had attracted her gaze.

WHEN I WAS A YOUNG BOY, THERE WERE MANY
celebrations in London. Most of them were to mark
various stages of the Boer War. This was a South African
War fought between Great Britain and the self-governing
Afrikaner or Boer colonies of the South African Republic
known as the Transvaal, and the Orange Free State. The
war started on October 11th 1899, after an ultimatum from
the Boer that the British should stop building up their
forces in that region. The war ended with a British victory
on May 31st, 1902, and there were many celebrations in
London to mark the occasion.

People particularly celebrated the relief of Mafeking, a
town which was besieged at the outbreak of the Boer War
in 1899, and at the end of the Siege of Ladysmith, a city
located to the south east of Johannesburg. The Siege of
Mafeking lasted 217 days from October 1899 until May
1900. The Siege of Ladysmith lasted 118 days from 2
November 1899 until 28 February 1900, during the most
crucial stage of the Boer War. Approximately 3,000
British soldiers lost their lives during the siege. People
placed candles in their homes, thousands of them, and
there were street parties and celebrations all around
London.

In 1901, when the soldiers returned home from the
war, we celebrated with a huge parade. Thousands of us
went to watch the soldiers march through Trafalgar
Square. The sound of cheering was terrific.

On the way back home after one of these occasions, I

heard a terrible row coming from a parked hansom cab. A very well-dressed couple were arguing quite vehemently. Suddenly, the lady took hold of the gentleman by his lapels and threw him out of the door of the cab! He went sprawling on the dirty road and his impressive top hat went spinning off into the distance. In those days the streets were pretty filthy, with horses pulling carriages everywhere and leaving behind their mess. It was also smelly, as you can imagine. The gentleman was lucky that he didn't land in anything nasty - I often wonder what he had done to deserve such treatment. The cab then sped off and left the man looking very embarrassed, sitting in the middle of the road. I'm sure he won't have forgotten that day in a hurry!

CHAPTER 4

NO ACCOUNTING FOR TASTE

The British farthing (1/4d) coin was a unit of currency of one quarter of a penny, or 1/960 of a pound sterling. It was minted in bronze, and replaced the earlier copper farthings. It was used during the reigns of six monarchs: Victoria, Edward VII, George V, Edward VIII, George VI and Elizabeth II, but ceased to be legal tender on 1 January 1961.

Before Decimal Day in 1971, there were 240 pence (plural of penny) in one pound sterling. There were four farthings in a penny, 12 pence made a shilling (also known colloquially as a 'bob'), and 20 shillings made a pound. Values less than a pound were usually written in terms of shillings and pence, e.g., three shillings and six pence (3/6), shortened to 'three and six' or 'three and sixpence'. Values of less than a shilling were simply written in pence, e.g., 8d - 'eightpence'. A price with a farthing in it would be written like this: (19/11+) - 'nineteen and elevenpence farthing'.

As a youngster I was given the princely sum of a

farthing each week as pocket money. As soon as I received it, I would run to one of the two sweet shops near my dad's shop. I wasn't a thrifty person at all back then! Mrs Clarke and Mrs Hall ran the two shops and they had a fine selection of bulls-eyes, coconut, pear and acid drops. I could afford an ounce of sweets with my weekly allowance. It was such a treat! Occasionally we would visit my grandmother, Caroline Major, who owned a sweet shop on Chiswick High Road, near Turnham Green. She ran it along with her daughter, my Aunt Maud. I loved to visit them, as they would always be sure to give me some free sweets! I'm still very partial to sweet things, especially mints, and always receive plenty of them as gifts for Christmas and my birthday each year.

My dad liked the odd drop of whisky in those days and this perfectly highlights how much prices have risen. Back then it only cost him two and sixpence (12 ½ p) for a bottle of whisky. If he felt like splashing out, there was also a deluxe version for three shillings (15 p). These days that wouldn't even buy you a sniff of the bottle! Government budgets always hit the pleasures of life, such as drinking and smoking. Long gone are the days you could get drunk for a shilling.

EVER SINCE I WAS A YOUNG BOY, MY FAVOURITE MEAL has been fish and chips. I very clearly remember every Saturday morning my mum packing up some drinks and sending all of us kids to Ravenscourt Park, with my sister Mabel looking after the baby in the pram. There were about five of us kids at the time, including the baby, and as soon as we were settled at the park with our picnic blanket laid out, I would be dispatched to the fish and chip shop on Beevor Lane in Hammersmith, to buy us four portions, which back then cost just sixpence. They knew exactly when I would be coming into the chippie, arriving as soon as possible after it opened at midday! We followed the same routine every week and they knew me by name. We would always have a friendly chat while I put salt and pepper on all of the portions. Back then I was able to eat an entire portion pretty quickly, but I've found the portions are getting too large for me these days.

So that the baby wouldn't fuss too much, our mum gave us an egg cup full of condensed milk to take with us to the park. If the baby started to cry we would dip the dummy into the condensed milk and that would put an end to the fussing. On one particular occasion, when I returned with the fish and chips, Mabel called to me, "Quick!", I hurried over to see what the problem was. Mabel had put the dummy into the baby's mouth and a horrible wasp was sitting right there on the dummy drinking the condensed milk from off the baby's lips! I was only seven or eight years old and really didn't know what to do. Mabel and I were panicking in case the wasp decided to sting the baby! Luckily the nasty creature flew away while we were still trying to decide what we ought to do!

ONE THING I STAYED WELL AWAY FROM EATING WAS BEEF dripping! Once, my sister Mabel and I were sent to the back of the West London Hospital with a bowl to collect beef dripping, which was given away at the kitchen door to poor families. Our father didn't want us to eat it on the way home, so he told us that it was collected from melting down all of the bodies of people who had died in the hospital! We were not sure if he was joking, but neither myself nor Mabel wanted to risk it!

CHAPTER 5
BORN ENTERTAINER

I have always loved to perform and I believe that my love of entertaining people began when I was a toddler. My family used to stage vaudeville shows to entertain the neighbours at our home in Hammersmith. At a very young age, my dad took me with him down to the local pub round the corner from the family business, The Ravenscourt Arms in Hammersmith, and stood me up on the bar to sing a few songs and entertain the other patrons. This was where I got my nickname of 'Jack' from. I'm not sure if it was after any particular performer or if they just thought it suited me better than Henry, but the patrons started to call me 'Jack' and it stuck. I'm still known as Jack to this day and if someone shouts out 'Henry!' it wouldn't occur to me to reply.

AFTER THAT EARLY BRUSH WITH FAME, WHICH I MUST have thoroughly enjoyed, I started to tell jokes when I was about twelve and by the time I was eighteen my friend

Harry Johnson and I had a little amateur act that we used to perform together. I loved music hall comedians and the way they could make ordinary stories seem funny. I used to go and watch them at the Hammersmith Palais on Shepherd's Bush Road, where they would have the entire audience in stitches with laughter. I tried to emulate this type of humour onstage, and it usually went down very well. One evening we had arranged to perform on stage at a place called the Hampshire Club, which was quite a fancy members club, whose members were leading Hammersmith tradesmen. The club paid well at 7s 6d, but they were very particular about the material performed there at the regular Saturday night shows. The man who booked us to perform told us that we couldn't use anything too 'blue', the term used for rude jokes at the time. He told us, "Anything too blue and we have a big hand which we will pull you off the stage with."

Harry and I were not worried about that because our act was clean, but there was some material which we had trouble with. We started a routine where Harry would hold up this photo of himself standing in the garden and ask me if I liked it. My answer was "Yes, but I don't like your pose." The punchline was then Harry saying, "They're not poes, they're flower pots, you fool." Poes was the word we used for chamber pots, which went under our beds for use if we needed the lavatory during the night.

Well, the mention of poes was too much for the Hampshire Club, the big hand came on and pulled us off the stage and we didn't get paid! What a shock to the system that was, but it taught me not to overstep the mark and to try and figure out what a particular audience will like as soon as possible after getting up onto the stage.

I THINK MY LOVE OF PERFORMING PROBABLY GOES HAND-in-hand with my love of visiting the theatre from a very early age, which I shared with my mother. My dear mum would get us free tickets every month for the two local theatres, The Empire and The Lyric Theatre, Hammersmith. Both of the theatres used to advertise their coming shows on posters which my father agreed to display in his shop window in exchange for free tickets in the stalls for my mother and me. No one else from the family was particularly interested in coming along with us, but this was my introduction to the wonderful world that is music hall and theatre. I loved going to watch and would get very involved in the melodramas and entertaining acts we would see and I still have some great memories of them. There would sometimes be an occasional mishap or unexpected interaction from the audience which would make the experience all the more enjoyable. We were watching the 'Grapes of Wrath' once, when one of the audience decided to intervene with the plot. The audience were all booing the evil villain and just at the moment when the nurse was on the verge of letting the main character drink from the poisoned cup, someone shouted out "Nurse, don't let him drink it, you fool, he's just poisoned it!" The audience erupted with cheers and applauded the audience member as if he were a hero. Luckily the actors were all able to keep their focus and go on with the show without collapsing in fits of laughter!

When we went to see 'The Midnight Mail', the heroine had been gagged and chained to the railway track by the villain and we could hear a train getting louder and louder from offstage as it approached her. We were all on the edges of our seats with the tension. Luckily the lady was saved just in the nick of time and the train appeared on stage, accompanied by thunderous sound effects. Unfortunately, the stage hands who were pushing the model train were a little too caught up in the action and kept on pushing until we could see them all on the stage, shoving the model train with all their might! They didn't realise they were on stage at first but when they heard the peals of laughter from the audience they soon cottoned on and rushed off stage in an embarrassed huddle.

Around Christmas time each year we would go and see a pantomime. When I was ten, it was Cinderella. As soon as I caught sight of the main actress with her long flowing blonde hair, I fell in love! I couldn't stop thinking about her after the show ended and the following day I found myself returning to the theatre and waiting by the stage door in the hopes of catching another glimpse of her. My head was full of her and I wanted to propose marriage! Unfortunately I didn't get the opportunity, there was no sign of the beautiful Cinderella and I had to go home disappointed and without a fiancée. Later I discovered she was already married to the actor who had been playing Buttons, so I'm glad I didn't embarrass myself by asking her for her hand in marriage. Never mind the fact that I was only ten at the time.

THE FAMILY THAT LIVED NEXT DOOR TO US IN Hammersmith had a son who earned a living as a music hall comedian. He used to have a bald wig as part of his act. At some point before the First World War, he got disgruntled with the theatrical life and decided that he was going to move to Australia. He knew how much I loved theatre and decided to give his bald wig to me as a parting gift. I loved it and immediately started using it in my act for some of the impersonations I did. I would put on the wig and sing the old Harry Champion song, 'Proud of me old bald head':

I'm Proud of My Old Bald Head

Written and composed by Murray - Collins:
Recorded 1911 by Harry Champion (1866-1942)

Some fellers when they lose their hair they fret
I've not started to worry yet
I used to have a lovely mop
Now I've got none on the top
You'd think with a cranium so bald catch a dreadful cough
I sometimes have a job to find out where my face leaves off
My parting's wide and so am I
Smack my old bald head and cry

Chorus: *Hair, hair, hair, I've got none on my noddle*
I don't care as down the street I toddle
All the people say, 'He's a good old thoroughbred.'

I never get the knock - I'm a jolly old cock
I'm proud of me old bald head

❧

The flies are very fond of it I think
It makes them a lovely skating rink
I polish it up with mutton fat
That's why I never wear a hat
Kids in the neighbourhood all shout out
'Ain't you lookin' bare
It makes you look half naked.'
But they can't shout out, 'There's hair.'
The girls they never let me pass
Makes them a lovely looking glass.

❧

Chorus: *Hair, hair, hair, I've got none on my noddle*
I don't care as down the street I toddle
All the people say, 'He's a good old thoroughbred.'
I never get the knock - I'm a jolly old cock
I'm proud of me old bald head

❧

While dining at the restaurant one night
I stooped and I had such a terrible fright
A girl stuck in my head a fork
Thought she'd dropped a slice of pork
As a youngster lots of water
On my brain they found
The hair fell in and couldn't swim

And that's how it got drowned
A chicken once sat on my thatch
My old bald head it tried to hatch.

Chorus: *Hair, hair, hair, I've got none on my noddle*
I don't care as down the street I toddle
All the people say, 'He's a good old thoroughbred.'
I never get the knock - I'm a jolly old cock
I'm proud of me old bald head

THE SONGS ALWAYS SEEMED TO GO DOWN BETTER WITH the audience when I wore the wig. I kept it for a long time and took it away to war with me. It featured in a fair amount of cabaret shows entertaining fellow troops, and I soon became quite well-known for having it. It was a difficult thing to have to carry around in my pack, though, and I preferred not to leave it anywhere, since we were often moved around at the front. I didn't want to lose my wig - it was a little piece of home that I had with me there in the trenches. I cleared a space for it in my haversack by getting rid of my hard tack biscuits, which were part of the emergency rations we soldiers were given. They had been crushed to dust, anyway, from being bashed by my tin of Bully Beef. I was very fond of that wig and hoped it would last until the end of the conflict. Indeed it may have, but unfortunately not with me! The last time I saw it was on my twenty-fourth birthday, the day of the final German offensive when I was taken prisoner and had to leave my belongings behind. Our haversacks were thrown into a pile which I assume the Germans then kept as souvenirs. I wonder what crossed their minds when they opened up my pack and found the bald wig and theatrical makeup! They may have thought British soldiers were crazy. Or maybe they took it and used it in their own concert parties. There might even be a German soldier somewhere writing his memoirs, with a chapter that starts 'I never understood why that haversack had a bald wig inside it…'

CHAPTER 6

CHILDISH PASTIMES IN PAST TIMES

I have been a lifelong fan of watching sports of any kind, and my first memory of watching a sport live revolves around the annual London boat race which went through Hammersmith on the River Thames from Putney to Mortlake. It is a 4.2 mile rowing race between Oxford and Cambridge University teams which began back in 1829 and is still held to this day, although they had to pause it during the First and Second World Wars. We would all dress up in our best clothes and head down to the river bank to watch the excitement along with thousands of other families, all jostling to get the best view from the bank of the River Thames! A fair few people would end up getting pushed and shoved into the river in all the excitement, I can tell you! As the boats came into view we would shout at the tops of our voices to encourage the rowers on whichever team we had decided to support that year. To this day, the Oxford Blues still wear navy blue jerseys whereas the Cambridge Blues are dressed in light blue.

ANOTHER SPORT I LOVED TO WATCH LIVE, AS A BOY, WAS football. I still love watching football matches on television, but unfortunately I'm unable to go to watch live games these days. My local team growing up was Brentford FC, whose club wasn't too far from where I lived in Hammersmith. I enjoyed watching them throughout my youth, through thick and thin. Unfortunately it was more thin than thick! The very first football match I went to was at Craven Cottage, home of Fulham FC, in 1903. Fulham FC was another team that was based very close to my home. I can no longer remember who they played that day, but I vividly remember being surrounded by a packed crowd of swaying supporters, who were chanting, and the feeling of excitement in the air. The ticket price back then was sixpence for adults, which was quite a lot of money. It was well worth it though for such a fantastic day out. During the winter games we would have a cup of Bovril beef tea to warm up our hands while we watched, as it could get pretty chilly standing outside for the duration of the game.

THE FIRST CINEMAS BEGAN TO OPEN IN HAMMERSMITH back in the early 1900s, when I was still a very young boy. We used to call them picture houses and I really enjoyed going to watch a film. It was a real treat, which we would save up our weekly allowance for and I would always be dumbfounded by the huge screen and the actors with their amazing range of facial expressions. In those early days there was no soundtrack to the movies and there would be a pianist who played along at the side of the screen. The dialogue was written in text on the screen between the action sequences. You had to concentrate pretty hard sometimes to figure out what was going on. As a result of this, the storylines tended to be quite simple but we loved them nevertheless.

The first 'talkie' I ever saw was 'Showboat' starring Paul Robeson, which opened in 1936. It was a musical set on a Mississippi river boat and I enjoyed it immensely. It was amazing to finally be able to hear the voices of the actors and actresses and to hear the dramatic music which accompanied the action. We would watch these films over and over and learn all the songs so that we could sing along to them in the picture house and also perform some of them at family parties and whenever we were entertaining people.

THERE WERE NUMEROUS SNOWY WINTERS WHEN I WAS growing up in London. Our street would be knee-deep and we would all have to go out and shovel away the snow in order to access our homes. We had so much fun - the snow was thick enough that it could be made into sturdy walls and we made tunnels through the drifts, connecting all the houses together like a rabbit warren. Whenever it snowed we kids would have a wonderful time getting up to mischief. There were a few times we managed to throw snowballs through house windows, by mistake. Well, that's my story and I'm sticking to it! I would always run off sharpish before getting caught by the poor unfortunate people who had to clean up the broken glass. I was a proper rascal! Whenever the conditions caused the River

Thames to freeze over we knew we were also going to be in for some fun ice skating. There was an especially good place for skating right near Hammersmith Bridge and we would spend hours out on the ice. It also worked as a useful shortcut to be able to cross the river that way, rather than having to go round to the bridge to cross. It didn't really occur to us how dangerous this would be if the ice had cracked, it was our winter playground and we loved it!

Winter had its downsides back in those days. Every year, the pipes would freeze. One time our street had so many burst pipes and connections that we had to be given standpipes out on the pavement so we could access water while everything was getting repaired. The early morning queue to fetch a couple of buckets full of water in the freezing cold was no fun at all, I can tell you!

One very upsetting occurrence, which happened far too frequently in the frigid temperatures, was when a horse would slip on the ice and fall down, breaking its leg. Back then, before cars, horses were the main method of transport, pulling carts and wagons behind them. A lot of owners couldn't spare the time to nurse the poor creatures back to health and would kill them there on the spot where they fell. They did this with a tool called a poleaxe, a club with a spike sticking out of the end, which they would use to hit the terrified animal between its eyes. The owner would then drag the animal away and dispose of its body. It was a heartless end for a loyal beast and a very disturbing sight.

CHAPTER 7

MISCHIEVOUS CHILD

At the tender age of five or six I discovered that my shoulders were actually wider than my head! I was a mischievous boy and would often get into scrapes, much to my poor mother's embarrassment and annoyance! One Christmas my mother had joined what was known as a 'Goose Club'. It was a kind of savings scheme whereby she would put a little money aside with the butcher each week before Christmas, for around thirteen weeks. We paid 6d per week at St. Peter's Boys' School. The money would earn you a goose or a turkey, some Dundee cake and the festive trimmings required for Christmas dinner, along with half a pound of tea. Finally the day came when we had saved up six shillings and sixpence and could go along to Palmer's Stores, the Butcher's Shop on King Street, Hammersmith to pick up our bounty. The Christmas geese and turkeys were all hanging outside, above the entrance to the shop and above the shop window in rows and rows. My mother went inside to ask the butcher to bring down a few of the birds, with his great stick which had a hook on it, so that she could pick the nicest looking one for our festive meal. This left me with not much to do and being a mischievous child I looked around to see what kind of trouble I could get into.

I quickly noticed a tree outside the shop, enclosed within a circle of six-foot railings, probably to keep the dogs away. I was eager to see if I could get through the railings to investigate the tree further and put my head through the tall black railings, thinking that if my head would fit through the gap between the railings, then so would the rest of me and that I would then be able to have some fun climbing the tree. My head just fit through the railings and, of course, that was as far as I could get. My shoulders would not follow, no matter how hard I tried. I tried to pull my head back out, but now my ears were in the way and I was unable to escape the railings. I began to panic, and started shouting for help, worried about the reaction I would get from my mother when she saw what silliness I had been getting up to. A crowd began to gather, attracted by my plaintive calls for help, and soon my mother came outside, accompanied by the butcher. They put their heads together to try and think how best to free me. In the end they decided there was no easy way to release me and it ended up needing the brute strength of the butcher. The railings were sturdy, but the butcher pulled up his sleeves and began tugging on them with all his might. This went on for quite a while until eventually they gave way, just a little, but just enough that I was able to slip my head out and jump back to safety. What a relief that was!

AROUND THIS TIME WE WERE STILL LIVING ABOVE MY
father's shop at Thomas Place, King Street, Hammersmith. A family of Jewish people lived across the road from
us, more or less directly opposite. On one occasion, one of
the elderly family members passed away and, as was their
tradition, a mute mourner was paid to stand outside their
front door all day. He wore black and spent the whole time
solemnly looking down at his feet. Since he was almost
directly opposite, I decided it would be great fun to use
this poor man as a target for pea-shooter practice from the
window of our living room! What a naughty scamp I must
have been. My poor mother certainly had her hands full
with a large family to look after and my antics to keep
under control! You would think that I would have learned
my lesson when it came to sticking my head through railings, from the embarrassing escapade outside the butcher's
shop, but I didn't. A few years later I was on my way from
Hammersmith over the bridge to Barnes and I noticed a
boat about to go under the bridge. I found myself on
Hammersmith Bridge craning my neck through the safety
railings, put there to stop people from falling off the
bridge into the River Thames, in order to watch the boat
on its way underneath. Again, as I tried to withdraw my
head, I found it had got stuck. My embarrassment on that
particular occasion was saved by a passing gentleman who
grabbed hold of me and pulled me out from between the
railings. After that I decided it would be best if I stayed
well away from all kinds of bars and railings!

ON ANOTHER OCCASION, WHEN MAKING MY WAY TO
Sunday School at St. Peter's School, Hammersmith, all

dressed up in my Sunday best, I got into trouble along the River Thames by Hammersmith Bridge. Along the way I ran into some boys who I knew, and they asked me to go with them over the Hammersmith Bridge, to the Barnes side, where there was a towpath which ran along the side of the river. The towpath was used by bargemen, who pulled barges along by attaching a rope to a horse walking along the towpath. Along that path there was an embankment which led straight down into the river, with nothing to protect you from falling in. It was made of funny old cobblestones separated occasionally by a set of steps down to the water's edge. I was just walking along the towpath with my friends, minding my own business, when suddenly one of the more boisterous of them gave me quite a hard push and I fell into the river! The current wasn't too strong at that time, and I was floating along, trying to hang onto the side of the riverbank. One of the biggest boys from our group, Ben Barge, luckily used his head and had the good sense to run down the next set of steps at the river's edge, and wait until the river brought me to him. Just as I got to him, he stuck out his leg for me to grab onto and I caught hold of his boot and hung on for dear life! Since I was only a little chap, he was able to pull me up until I was on the steps, and safe again! He probably saved my life, as I did not know how to swim at that point. I had to go back home soaked to the skin in my sopping wet Sunday clothes and, once there, got into trouble with my mother all over again!

CHAPTER 8

WILD WEST LONDON

At around the same time, when I was about six, my parents started to take me to the fair at Earl's Court in West London. It was a huge travelling fair which came once a year, and we all loved to go. It stayed in town for a month and it cost sixpence to get in. I had to save up the money from my errands in order to afford the entrance fee, but I didn't mind, as I loved to go on the fairground rides and see all the attractions on offer. I loved the coconut shy, where you threw fairly large wooden balls at a coconut on a stand and if you could knock it to the ground you got to keep the coconut, but the first few years I went, I found the balls were too heavy for me to lift, never mind trying to throw them!

Some of the fairground rides went up in the air, higher than a hundred feet and I didn't like the thought of those, as I've never liked heights. What I did enjoy, though, was when the small boys would buy water guns for a penny. It was fun dodging the young rascals as you walked around the stalls, so as not to get soaked to your skin when they targeted you.

There was a renowned 'Fat Lady' in a tent who people would pay a penny to have a look at. I could never really understand this, since the stallholder would show you pictures of the poor woman to help entice you in. Surely this would mean you didn't need to pay to enter the tent, as you'd already seen her!

One year the main attraction at the fair was a Wild West Show, featuring none other than the famous Buffalo Bill Cody. He was an enormous man with long fair hair tucked up inside a large-brimmed hat and he had a big droopy moustache. He looked just like the photos I'd seen of him. The rodeo show he put on was extremely popular - after all how often do you get to see someone lasso a bucking calf in the middle of the High Street? There were a number of horsemen in his rodeo show and they were all highly skilled, clambering all over the backs of their horses as they galloped around the ring at incredible speed. It looked as if the riders were certain to fall off and break their necks, but it was highly exciting to watch. During their performance, the riders even crawled underneath their horses, before returning onto their backs to continue riding around the ring. The next year I was at the front of the queue for a ticket when their Wild West show returned. They were so daring and flamboyant - I wanted to be just like them when I grew up. Unfortunately, there wasn't much call for that kind of cowboy in west London!

CHAPTER 9

TRAVELLING ON THE TUBE

A t around the age of six, I had another interesting outing, when I was lucky enough to be one of the first people to travel on the Central London Railway (CLR), on its opening day. It was opened to the public on July 30th 1900, and went from Shepherd's Bush station to Bank station. Everyone was very excited about the prospect of a train travelling through tunnels underneath the city, and running on electricity, too! When my father decided we would be among the first to ride on the new railway from Shepherd's Bush station I could barely contain my excitement! He told me that a prominent politician had opened the railway route earlier that day, the same day we were going to travel!

Our adventure began when we arrived at the station and had to take a lift down to the level under the ground where the train tracks had been installed. It was a little scary to be going so far beneath the city. In those days there were no escalators, or 'moving stairways' as we called them. It was just lifts and everyone had to wait for the lift to ascend once more before climbing aboard. Being a small boy, I couldn't see very much among the crowds of eager people, but I remember the sensation of descending into the depths of the Earth! As we spilled out of the lift, I was amazed to see how long the platforms were. The tunnel from which the train was expected to appear was like a giant gaping mouth. It then occurred to me how the underground railway got its nickname of the 'Twopenny Tube'. The tickets cost two pence for a journey between any two stations and the tunnels, with their sleek curved walls did indeed look like tubes. It didn't matter if you were travelling all the way to Bank, or getting off somewhere earlier, it was still just two pence for a ticket. Suddenly I heard the noise of the train approaching and was transfixed as the noise got louder and louder until - whoosh! - out of the tunnel came the train, thundering towards us at breakneck speed. It was a marvellous sight! The doors were automatic, which was something we had never seen before. It was as though they opened and closed by magic! You had to be quick getting on the train though, before they swished shut behind you.

Our destination was Bank station, some twelve miles and half an hour's journey away. The train stopped along the way at Holland Park, Notting Hill Gate, Queen's Road (now Queensway), Lancaster Gate, Marble Arch, Oxford Circus, Tottenham Court Road, British Museum (closed in 1933), Chancery Lane, Post Office (now called St. Paul's). Bond Street Station was also on the line, but was opened a few months later in September 1900.

We squeezed ourselves onto the train and off we went. All the seats were occupied on that first journey, because so many people were eager to try out the new train. I stood and clung to the back of a seat, as there was no way I could reach the leather straps that were suspended from the ceiling of the carriage for standing passengers to hang onto. As we went on our way I stared out of the windows into the tunnel and every so often the blackness was replaced by a flash of bright colour and lights as we entered a station. There were posters and billboards everywhere in the stations advertising the popular newspapers of the time, such as The Express, Daily Mail and Lloyds Weekly News. I also saw adverts for theatres and their latest music hall acts. It was all so exciting!

After what seemed like ages we eventually reached our destination, but it was only about half an hour. My father and I wandered out into the daylight, dazzled by the brightness. It's amazing to think that despite an enormous amount of development to the underground railway system those same stations are still in use so many years later. I wonder how many millions of passengers there have been since my first trip back in 1900. The line is now referred to simply as the Central Line, part of the London Underground.

The tunnels of the underground railway stations were also used by people during the Second World War as a safe place to shelter whenever there was a bombing raid. The stations were transformed into air raid shelters and crowds of Londoners would collect on the escalators, on the platforms and even on the train tracks, trying to keep safe.

CHAPTER 10
MONEY WOES

From a very early age, my parents taught me the value of saving money. From about the age of seven, I wanted my own savings account.

Back then, the Post Office was running a savings scheme whereby you saved up pennies and exchanged them for red stamps which you then fixed onto a form given to you by the Post Office. When you had twelve stamps, you could open a childrens' savings account.

It took me quite a long time to save twelve pennies, since the only real way I could earn money was by running errands for neighbours or helping my dad by delivering the shoes he had repaired. I got very excited every time I had a penny and could go to the Post Office to swap it for one of the glossy red stamps. Finally I had twelve stamps and was so proud of myself that I couldn't wait to take my completed form off to the Post Office and open the long awaited account.

It was a quarter of a mile from home. I put my form safely in my pocket and set off, really excited to become a bank customer on my own merit. I was almost all the way there when I checked my pocket to make sure the form was still there and discovered it had gone! I was horrified! I think it was one of the worst moments of my childhood, after all the time and effort I had spent saving.

There was no point in me going inside the Post Office without the form so I headed back towards home, scanning the pavement the whole time in the hope of finding the form. I walked home with tears in my eyes and told my father what had happened. He advised me to retrace my steps and keep looking for the form. His confidence that all was not lost gave me some hope, so off I went again, peering closely at the pavement as I went. I scoured the street at a snail's pace and noticed a small white packet as I once more approached the Post Office. Clearly it wasn't my form, but maybe there was something of interest inside it.

I picked it up and discovered a coin inside. It was half a crown, which was worth more than twice as much as the form I had lost. It was wrapped in a shopping list for the butcher and had probably been dropped by some poor soul doing an errand for their mother. I wasted no time in using the half crown to open my account and reassured myself that the person who lost the money had probably found my lost form.

That day taught me an important lesson, be more careful with the items I valued!

CHAPTER 11
ASCOT - THE SPORT OF KINGS

Every year in the summer we looked forward to the world famous horse-racing event known as Royal Ascot, named after the town in which it was held and the fact that the Royal family attended the races on the first day. It took place in late June and early July, and the town of Ascot, on the outskirts of London, was not far from where my family lived in Hammersmith.

Us children would gather excitedly in the streets to watch as a stream of horse-drawn coaches called 'brakes' left King Street and took hundreds of Hammersmith residents off along the Great West Road to the races to rub shoulders with the aristocracy. Each of the local pubs organised a coach for its customers and hired a photographer for the day. The photographer took a big team picture of the forty or so racing enthusiasts who were going to represent that particular pub. Everyone wanted to look their best, so they hired a top hat from Dunn & Co stores in Hammersmith. They would all have a buttonhole flower arrangement, and the resulting photo, taken outside the pub, would be publicity for the pub and quite a memento for everyone involved. Once the photo had been taken they would all climb back up into the brake via the spiral staircase at the back. The brakes were much like the open-topped buses you can see in London today, only back then they were drawn by horses. In addition to the driver, each bus had a trumpeter. For the entire journey to Ascot, he played all the popular music hall tunes, so everyone could happily sing along on the journey. Twenty or more pubs would arrange these brakes and it made for an amazing sight as they all formed a convoy and made their way to the races. We would hear them coming from the schoolyard and rush out onto the street to wave at them and cheer them on their way.

WE ONCE HEARD A STORY OF A POOR LADY WHO HAD recently lost her husband and the only photograph she had of him was one of these 'team' pictures taken outside a pub. She took it along to the local photographic studio to ask if they would be able to remove everyone else from the photo and also take off her husband's top hat, which she had never liked him wearing, in order to make a keepsake portrait for her. The photographer replied that he would be happy to do so and asked her for some details that would help him with the reproduction. He asked her "On what side did your husband part his hair?" The woman was rather taken aback. "Well," she replied, "when you take off his hat, you'll see for yourself!"

CHAPTER 12
COUNTRY ESCAPADES

When I was a mischievous ten-year-old my parents scraped together sixpence each week for months to send me on a country holiday to a kind of camp located at a big house with lots of other youngsters, in Amersham, Buckinghamshire. Amersham wasn't very far from where we lived but for a ten-year-old, going away without my family was a real adventure! I was only there for a week, but I managed to get into plenty of scrapes.

First of all I went paddling in a duck pond and managed to badly gash my foot on some sharp stones at the bottom. I went back into the house to get it bandaged up and then raced straight back outside again, having decided to climb a tree in order to pick some apples. I was quite good at climbing and reached the top of the tree fairly quickly and easily. When I got to the top, however, I slipped and fell. As it happened, the waistband of my breeches got tangled in a branch and saved me from crashing down to the ground! My breeches got badly torn and I was left dangling from the tree, upside down, literally hanging by a thread! Luckily, some of my chums noticed and came to rescue me. I didn't have any spare clothes with me, so unfortunately I had to stay inside the house, in my tattered breeches, until my parents could be contacted and asked to send me another pair. That was very frustrating, I can tell you, having to stay indoors while my friends were all out and about enjoying the sunshine and having more escapades, but I soon got back into the thick of things when my new breeches arrived! My mother was not happy with the state of my attire and I received quite a telling off that day! Being poor we didn't own many clothes and such accidents meant that our clothes were patched until they consisted more of patches than of original material!

CHAPTER 13
AN AUSTRALIAN VISITOR

When I was about ten-years-old, a stranger came to the door of our house in Thomas Place and introduced himself to my father as Tom Bain from Australia, my father's nephew. He was the son of Alice Bain, my father's older sister, who had emigrated to Australia in the 1860s when my father was still a small boy. We spent the evening chatting with him. He told us that his parents had sent him on a world tour to complete his education and that he had really wanted to meet some of his British family. Aunt Alice and her husband had made a fortune buying and reselling land in Queensland, Australia and with the proceeds had bought the ownership of a newspaper in Brisbane. Tom was planning to become a lawyer and showered us, his relatively downtrodden relatives, with gifts! After that evening we never heard of him again until much later when we were sent a copy of Alice Bain's obituary, which had been printed in 1933 in the 'Brisbane Courier-Mail' newspaper. It stated that Mrs Alice Maud Bain, who died at the age of eighty-three in her residence, 'Gowrie', on Wickham

Terrace was a native of Southampton, England, and had
gone to Brisbane with her husband Mr Robert Bain in
1869. Soon after their arrival in the colony, Mr and Mrs
Bain left Ipswich on a long coach journey to Charleville.
Hard pioneering experience on several well-known
stations followed. They decided to go overland to Victoria,
and bought a covered waggon for the purpose, but the
plans were changed, and Mr and Mrs Bain went to Brisbane, where Mrs Bain entered into business. In 1882 she
moved from Tollerton House, Charlotte Street, to the
house on Wickham Terrace, which she had had specially
built for her business, and in which she resided up to the
time of her death.

WHAT I DIDN'T REALISE AT THE TIME WAS THAT AN
amazing coincidence would happen in 1918, when I was in
the prisoner of war camp in Münster. I got to know a
couple of Australian prisoners from Brisbane. I thought I
would ask them if they happened to know of the newspaper and to my absolute surprise they not only knew of it,
but were also quite well-acquainted with my aunt and
uncle! They referred to her as 'Old Mother Bain, the Old
Lady of Wickham Terrace' and she was by then a well-
known character, one of the most influential and pros-
perous people in Brisbane. What a small world we live in!

CHAPTER 14
SCHOOL DAYS

I thoroughly enjoyed school and found both numbers and words fascinating. Geography was my favourite lesson, though. I loved to feel like I was travelling somewhere miles away on the other side of the planet, as we learned about far-flung places. I was a pretty bright student, though I say so myself, and, when I was attending St Peter's Boys' School on King Street, Hammersmith, I was very excited about a school prize ceremony. There were a lot of local dignitaries from the school governors' board in attendance, including William Bull, the Conservative Member of Parliament for Hammersmith. I ended up winning about seven separate prizes of books for doing well in my lessons, which made me very proud of myself.

My hand would shoot straight up, eagerly, always ready to answer the teachers' questions in class. Due to my unrelenting keenness, sometimes the teachers would want to give the other students a chance and would say, "Not you, Rogers!"

THERE WERE A FAIR NUMBER OF RASCALS IN MY CLASS. Two of the most mischievous were Boss Pepper and Charles Wilkinson. A practical joke they played one day was to block the chimney above the fire, which heated the entire school building. They smoked out the whole school and we missed some lessons while the poor caretaker tried to figure out what was happening with the fire he had just recently lit. Another time those same two rascals tied tin cans to the school bell which was rung to let us know when it was time for us to come to school. It made a very strange noise that day, with those cans tied to it. It was a very strict school and pupils got caned with a bamboo walking cane for such bad behaviour.

One day Titch Gathercole was called up in front of everyone to receive a caning, not on his hand as usual, but on his backside. The teacher was walloping him and Titch reached across and grabbed another nearby cane and started to hit the teacher back! It was very funny for those of us watching, but poor old Gathercole got a few extra wallops on his behind for his trouble!

EVERYONE AT SCHOOL HAD A NICKNAME. MINE WAS Fatty Rogers, because of my size. I only really lost the extra weight when I joined the army. Years later, when I was working on the window display of my shoe repair shop, I noticed a man suddenly stop and start intently watching me from outside the window. Then I heard a voice shout "Hello, Fat!". It was Alf Sellen who I had sat next to at school all those years ago. I hadn't heard that nickname for many years! We had a good old reminisce about those school days together. The happiest days of our lives!

CHAPTER 15

HAUNTED HOUSE?

There was a large house on Ravenscourt Park called Hamlet House, which used to scare the living daylights out of us all when we were kids. It was a kind of legend in our part of London when I was a boy, with a reputation of being haunted. Its large grounds backed onto the railway line, which ran between Hammersmith and Hounslow. Us kids would try to avoid walking past the place if we could, but my father did a lot of shoe repairing for customers in that part of town, so unfortunately I was sent to deliver the mended shoes back to their owners. During the winter this often ended up happening in the dark, and I would walk down Ravenscourt Park, feeling terrified as I approached Hamlet House. I would cross the street and walk on the other side to avoid it, all the while my imagination playing tricks on me. I would keep my eyes fixed on the place as I walked along, hoping not to see any ghosts or ghouls reaching out with menacing fingers from behind the railings to grab me. The house had just one mysterious inhabitant, an aged caretaker who was hardly ever seen and this added to the creepy feeling. He had a dog which you could hear howling like a wolf and making other strange noises, but would never catch sight of.

Over the years the house fell further into disrepair and eventually became derelict. It was then bought by a film company who converted it into a film studio which was very welcome to the locals, since we could get work there as film extras and were paid £ 1 per day. That was a lot of money back then, before the First World War broke out. A postman was paid around 18 bob a week, and a policeman received about 22 bob a week (a bob is equivalent to about five pence) .

Getting picked to be an extra wasn't easy. Queues would form by the gates first thing in the morning as soon as everyone heard that the film company needed people. We were very lucky one day, because my friend heard that a lot of people would be needed for one particular scene they were filming. Our ambition was to become world famous stars of the silver screen, so we went down there straight away to try our luck. We were delighted when they chose us and felt sure it was the beginning of a shiny new career in the movies, with all of the fame and fortune that could bring! We went inside the gates and proceeded to stroll around the garden, acting like minor stars in the background of the shot they were filming. At this point we had long forgotten any qualms we had about the house being haunted. We were only needed for two hours in the end and didn't see anyone famous or even find out the name of the film that was being made, so I have absolutely no idea if I even got to be on screen! At least it gave me the opportunity to stop thinking of that house as a scary place to be avoided like the plague! The last thing I heard about it was that it had been converted into a launderette. I wonder if people hear howling dogs and see ghosts come wafting out of the washing machines at them, while they are doing their laundry.

CHAPTER 16

A FREQUENTER OF PUBS FROM
AN EARLY AGE!

My father's favourite pubs were the Ravenscourt Arms, The Doves by the River Thames, and The Gardeners Arms on King Street, Hammersmith. The rent for our home and for the shop at Thomas Place was seven shillings (the equivalent of 35 pence - which was a fairly large amount of money), and was due each Monday. As a young child of seven or eight, I used to be sent round those three pubs, looking for my father to get the rent money from him and take it to the collector's office, Pascalls, near Thomas Place. I saw some sights during my visits to those pubs which were not meant for a boy of my tender age, I can tell you! In addition to these pubs, when he could walk well my father would sometimes go as far as Brentford to go drinking, which meant I would have a much longer walk to go and find him. As his health began to suffer and he needed to be wheeled around in a bath chair (a wheelchair, popular at the time, made from wicker, named for the reclining position its user finds themselves in, similar to lying back in a

bath) it became my job to go and fetch him from whichever pub he was in between 10.00 p.m. and 11.00 p.m. and
wheel him back home again.

CHAPTER 17

OUR NEIGHBOUR, SIR WILLIAM BULL

From 1900 until 1918, the Conservative Member of Parliament for Hammersmith was Sir William Bull. He later became Member of Parliament for Hammersmith South, after some boundary changes were introduced. He remained in this position of local governmental power until 1929. He ran a solicitor's business, from offices just around the corner from my father's boot and shoe repair shop, and I would often see this local celebrity when I was out pushing my father around in his bath chair before setting off for school. He would greet my father with a booming, "Good morning, Rogers!" From time to time I also encountered him at school, as he was one of the governors at St. Peter's and he would regularly visit for our prize-giving ceremony at Christmas and on other occasions, to keep an eye on how we were all progressing. Whenever he was due to visit our school the teachers made certain we were on our best behaviour.

Sir William was well-recognised in Hammersmith. I even had the opportunity to work in his offices as a junior trainee, but because of my father's failing health that was never able to happen. Back in the 1900s he was the first member of parliament to suggest a channel tunnel between England and France. To begin with the idea didn't get very far, but his so-called 'wild' ideas have since been vindicated. The Channel Tunnel which now runs between Folkestone, Kent, UK and Coquelles, France was finally opened in May 1994, a long time after Sir William's original suggestions! I have never travelled through it, but imagine it to be quite a scary experience knowing you are travelling under the weight of the sea with no real escape if something should go wrong! Mind you I am fairly claustrophobic these days.

As I mentioned, Sir William's offices were only a few doors away from our family boot and shoe repair business. Rumour had it that they were built on the site of an old plague burial pit. There was a big statue of a bull outside the offices, under which were the words 'Hither To', which I understand was his family's motto. The statue lent an imposing air to the building. One time, when I was about five years old, he sent a message out to all the local shopkeepers and business owners that one of his clients, a very rich lady, had lost a diamond from her ring while visiting his offices and that he was prepared to offer a reward to anyone who could locate the missing precious stone. My father sent me out looking for what he called a sparkly stone. I wanted to please my dear old dad so I tried really hard to find it, unaware of the value of the item for which I was searching. Would you believe that I managed to find it? It was really quite small and I clenched it tightly in my fist so that I wouldn't lose it until I could present it to my amazed father, back at the shop. I really am blessed with good fortune, aren't I? I can't remember ever receiving the reward, but I'm sure my dad must have received it on my behalf and kept it safe for me.

QUITE A FEW YEARS LATER, I REMEMBER SEEING A LARGE group of people marching down the road and stopping off at the big bull statue outside Sir William's offices. It was toward the end of their march and I would say there were around 200 of them, having marched from the north of England over the course of three weeks. This was one of the 'hunger marches' which was a precursor to the Jarrow March of 1936. These marches were mainly arranged by the National Unemployed Workers Movement (NUWM) and were protesting post war unemployment. It was quite a sight to behold! The marchers were obviously Labour supporters, but I remember he gave each of them a shilling to go and buy themselves some food and a pint of beer, for which they all gave him a hearty cheer.

PART III
TEENAGE YEARS

M y father suffered terribly from chalk gout, a nasty disease of the feet and hands which he may have inherited from his father, Edward, who was also a sufferer, as was his sister Alice Bain. His joints would swell up and he would burst out in great blisters, which meant he was unable to walk, so my siblings and I had to push him around in a bath chair (a wicker wheelchair). There was nothing the doctors of the day could do for him so he just got increasingly worse. There was no treatment for his illness, but he finally found a medicine which contained opium, which gave him some relief from the constant pain. Due to my father's ill health I was persuaded to take my school leaver's matriculation exams at the tender age of thirteen, in 1907. I then left school to go and work full-time in Dad's shop, 'Rogers & Son'. I learned how to repair and make shoes from leather, and could refer to myself as a cobbler, a profession which would come to be a life-saving skill when I found myself in a prison camp during the First World War. I have always regretted having to leave school early, but I was used to hanging around at my dad's shop, as I had been helping him out with deliveries for many years already and felt quite at home there.

As it was such a long street, King Street was split into two halves, for the purposes of the local constabulary. One half between Weltje Road and Young's Corner and the other from Weltje Road to Hammersmith Broadway. There were two police constables, one assigned to 'walk the beat' on each half of the street and we would see each of them regularly, as they patrolled up and down during their four hour shifts. One of the bobbies was PC Grant, who had grown up near my father in the Southampton area, and he always used to pop into our shop for a sit down and a chat with my dad in the little room at the back of the shop, which was cordoned off by a little curtain.

He would come marching in like he owned the place, stride to the back of the shop, take off his boots and helmet and put his feet up on the table! Then it would often not be long before he fell asleep. I thought he was a bit of a pain in the neck, because he always seemed to be there, and sometimes he brought his colleagues along with him. They were supposed to be patrolling for their four-hour shift, but instead they were hidden away in the back of our shop having an unscheduled break, a gossip and an afternoon nap! Sometimes PC Grant even sent me to the local pub to pick up tankards of ale. Luckily, I was able to get served in the pub because they recognised me from being in there with my father, despite the fact that I was well under the drinking age of the time!

The only problem with this ruse of theirs was that their superior officer, a fierce Scotsman called Sergeant McPherson, would often be found out on the streets of Hammersmith, checking that his constables were adhering to their assigned rounds, as expected. He was a stickler for efficiency and a bit tyrannical. PC Grant decided that it could be my job to keep him informed on the whereabouts of his superior and kept sending me out to check if the coast was clear.

On one particular occasion PC Grant had already been sitting in the shop with us for an hour when he sent me out for a look around at about 8 p.m. I wandered up King Street, and sure enough there was Sergeant McPherson. I quickly ran back to the shop.

Due to his ill health, my father was in his bath chair by this point, so I shut up shop, turned off the lights and wheeled him out of the front door and up the road towards the sergeant. We bid him a goodnight and continued until we had gone around the corner, where I parked my father's chair out of sight and then waited for the sergeant to move on past our shop. Then, I rushed back to the shop to let out PC Grant, who we had had to lock inside. Off he scurried, back to his beat, as if nothing had happened, narrowly missing being seen by his superior, and luckily getting away with his scam.

Jack Rogers outside 'Rogers & Son' around 1909.

CHAPTER 19
CYCLING PROFICIENCY

W hen I was about fourteen, I was given a bike by our neighbour, Mr Bailey, who lived in the bottom half of our house in Goldhawk Road. It was an ordinary black bicycle with a bell and lamps. Unfortunately it was too big for me, since it was a full-sized adult bike and I only had little legs, being a bit short. I had to ride it with the saddle removed and replaced by a makeshift seat, which I made out of some old rags, wrapping them around the saddle post for comfort. Mr Bailey was about eighty years old and had his own business repairing bicycles, children's prams and bath chairs. He was always busy and I would often run errands to help him out. This was why he gave me the bike, which someone had left in his shed. I soon became very fond of it.

One day he asked me to deliver a bath chair he had been fixing to its owner, a lady who lived in Hanwell, six miles up the Uxbridge Rd. He had the bright idea of hooking the chair up to the back of the bike with the handle sticking out and me towing it all the way to the customer's house, for which he would pay me half a crown.

I invited my sister Nell along for the ride. We must have made an amusing sight with me on the bike, pedalling my heart out, and Nell sitting behind, relaxed in the bath chair! Everything was going well on the straight but when we reached the hill just after Ealing Common I was so tired that I had to get off the bike and push it, with Nell pushing the bath chair along behind. At the top of the hill, near Sion Lane, we had a rest and I noticed an apple tree growing on the other side of a wall nearby. Always full of mischief, I decided it would be a good idea to climb over the wall and fill my pockets with apples to share with the rest of my family later. Just as I was making my getaway, with pockets laden with apples, a great big vicious-looking guard dog came out of nowhere and chased me. I had to run so fast I managed to lose all of the apples in the process! I've never scrambled over a wall quite as fast, I could hear the dog growling right behind me as I ran and was certain he would take a bite of my behind at any moment!

Nell and I set off again down the other side of the hill, which, with the help of gravity, was much easier going. The bath chair was going faster than the bike and kept banging into me as we went along, nearly knocking me off my makeshift saddle. Somehow I managed to remain seated until we got to our destination, where the customer was happy to see her bath chair and gave me a shilling as a tip.

Once we had delivered the chair we realised there was a problem. How were we going to get Nell home? She didn't want to walk all that way, and we only had one bike. We hadn't really thought the whole thing through prop- erly. Luckily the bike had two pieces of metal, probably screws, on either side of the back wheel which she was able to balance on, albeit in a precarious fashion. We wobbled our way safely home like this and again must have been quite something to behold for anyone out and about in the vicinity of Hammersmith and Hanwell that day.

A few years later I had to part company with that trusty iron steed in unfortunate circumstances..

☙❧

WE WERE LIVING IN A BIGGER HOUSE IN DORVILLE Road by then, and my sisters attended the Paddenswick Road Free School for girls. Four of my sisters were going to travel by tram on a school trip to Hampton Court Palace, just up the River Thames from where we lived. This outing happened annually during the summertime, and an old tram would pick up the girls from school. After spending half a day at Hampton Court Palace, they would be taken into the Old Deer Park which faced the palace, where there would be a marquee set up in which they were given a free tea. After teatime was over the tram would bring them back to their school in Hammersmith.

In 1914, I decided that the girls shouldn't be the only ones to partake in this fun summer's day out and so I thought I would follow along, behind the tram with my bike, for the twelve miles, and meet them at the other end of their journey for a nice cup of tea and a pleasant afternoon. Everything was going swimmingly with me following behind the tram, and the girls sitting at the back cheering me on. We had a lovely time at Hampton Court, but then, when we were travelling home again, disaster struck! The girls were all at the back of the London United Electric Tram again, waving at me as I cycled after them. I was bobbing and weaving along the road and suddenly, a little

way outside of Hampton Court, a vehicle had got stuck
somehow and I had to swerve around it on my bike. My
wheel got stuck in the tram track and I came a real crop-
per! I skidded along the road and my leg was torn up
painfully by the rough surface and my trousers ripped to
pieces. The poor bike was mangled beyond repair. My
unhappy sisters could do nothing but watch fearfully as
the tram took them away from their injured brother.

Since my bike was ruined, I had to push what was left
of it and painfully limp the rest of the way back home - a
distance of almost ten miles - with my clothes ruined.
When the girls reached home and told my parents what
had happened they didn't know what to do for the best! It
was already evening by then. They went across
Paddenswick Road to the Police Section House and
explained what had happened and asked the police to telephone the local hospitals in case I had been taken to one
of them as a casualty. But the hospitals had no record of
such an accident. I finally reached home around 3.00 a.m.
the next morning, but I was so glad when I did, covered in
blood and exhausted as I was! What a lovely day out that
had proved to be! I was in no hurry to join them on any
future adventures!

THE NEXT BIKE I BOUGHT WAS A NEW FIXED-WHEEL
bike, and with it I decided I would become a member of a
local cycling club. It was fantastic; we used to cycle from
London to Brighton whenever there was a bank holiday
and would stay down there for the weekend. We had a
wonderful time in Brighton, flirting with girls and getting
up to mischief on the pier. Our last ride down to Brighton

was a very memorable one for me. The date was August 4th, 1914, the day the First World War broke out. As soon as we got back from Brighton, most of the cycling club signed up to fight. Out of twenty cycling club members, I only ever saw three again. The others were all victims of the Great War.

CHAPTER 20

SPORTING PURSUITS

Before war broke out, one of my favourite pastimes was going dancing at the Hammersmith 'Palais de Dance' in Brook Green Road. I could be found there on most Saturday nights, tripping the light fantastic to the sounds of the Big Band leaders, such as Joe Loss and Edmundo Ross. Each year they staged a very popular event, where local songwriters were invited to write a tune for a competition and the winning entry was performed by Joe Loss and his band. That was quite an honour back then as Joe Loss was very famous. My friends and I would dress up in our finest clothes and hope that perhaps we would pluck up the courage to talk to a girl and ask her to dance.

IN ADDITION TO DANCING, I ALSO USED TO LIKE TO GO rowing as a teenager. Having watched the Boat Race every year of my childhood and living so close to the River Thames, it was probably inevitable that sooner or later I would try my hand at it myself. My friend and soon to be brother-in-law, Will Price, and I, would often go rowing on the River Thames. We would hire a two-man scull from a place called Biffen's Boathouse, which was located right next to Hammersmith Bridge, on the river. Usually we went out for an hour's exercise and kept track of the time using the clocks on the two churches along our route. One day we noted our departure time on the clock at St Paul's Church as being 11 o'clock and off we went towards the Black Lion steps, which took their name from the nearby pub. Our next time check was from the bottom of those steps, looking at the clock on the nearby St Peter's church, about half a mile downstream. Well, on one particular occasion, time was playing tricks with us, we saw that the time was now 10.55 am. We had traveled half a mile and got there five minutes before we set off! "That was quick wasn't it?" Will said and we had a good laugh about it, wondering if our fast rowing time would have allowed us to qualify for the team that took part in the 1912 Olympics! We knew we were getting fit with all our regular training but hadn't realised we had got so speedy that we could go back in time!

A young Jack Rogers (on the right) taken at King Street,
Hammersmith, probably on boat race day around 1911.
With Jack is Will Price, who later became Jack's
brother-in-law.

I ALSO REMEMBER THE DAY AN AMERICAN SPORT MADE
its way to our little corner of the world. There had been
posters all over the area, advertising the impending excitement for weeks. The Chicago White Sox baseball team
were going to be taking on the New York Giants at Stamford Bridge, the home of Chelsea Football Club. We
couldn't wait - real live baseball right here in our backyard,
it was so exciting! It was a charity match and everyone was
eager to go. There was no way I was going to miss this, so
bright and early, I queued up excitedly at Stamford Bridge
in order to buy my ticket.

We were giddy with anticipation and luckily our seats
were high up on one of the terraces, so I could see and
hear everything quite clearly, including hearing a number
of American accents mixed in among the crowd of specta-
tors. Over 30,000 people showed up to watch the game!
We were glued to the action playing out in front of us, and
were amazed by the sheer size of the players. They were
called The Giants for a good reason! The team from
Chicago wore their traditional white socks which gave

them their team name and the Giants were dressed all in blue uniforms. We were amazed by their strength as they hit the ball all over the place with bats which seemed enormous to us. The fielders were equally impressive, hurling the ball back from the outer field with remarkable strength. We were awestruck by the strange actions the pitchers would use, seeming to wind themselves up in knots and then kicking their legs so that they could unwind themselves and throw the ball with unbelievable speed in the direction of the batter. It was a fantastic day out and an unforgettable spectacle. I'm surprised it didn't really take off in this country as a sport.

CHAPTER 21
'GREASY' RUSSIANS

I loved cycling and travelling around the countryside when I was younger. One time my mate Ernie White and I were on a cycling holiday in Portland, Dorset just before the First World War broke out. We had caught the train to Dorset from Paddington station, bringing our bikes with us. After we had been there a few days and felt settled in, we decided we would like to get a haircut, nothing special, just a simple short back and sides. We found the barber shop but it appeared to be closed. There was nobody around, even though it was the middle of the day and a weekday. We couldn't understand why there was no reply when we knocked on the door, since it wasn't an early closing day or a Bank Holiday (Wednesdays in the UK were half days known as Early Closing Days, to allow a break for workers who often toiled seven days each week). We tried again but still there was no sign of life. Suddenly, when we had just about given up, a man's bald head appeared above the door curtain. The head belonged to the barber. He carefully opened the door and peered around us before asking what we wanted. I thought that it was pretty obvious we wanted a haircut since we had come to a barbershop, but I kept those thoughts to myself and politely answered him. He quickly let us in and then proceeded to lock the door behind us. He asked us to stay down out of sight of anyone who might look through the window. We couldn't understand what was going on. What strange behaviour! But after all we were from London, perhaps this was how people did business in Dorset! It was all very intriguing so we were pleased when he explained his unusual antics to us. Apparently there were a couple of Russian battleships anchored in Portland harbour and he was worried we might be Russian sailors. The town had been receiving a steady stream of Russians on shore leave and large groups of them had been visiting his barbershop and stealing his supplies of Brilliantine scented hair oil. One or two of the sailors would keep him busy asking in broken English for a haircut and the others would be brazenly pinching his stock from off his shelves! There was nothing like it in Russia, apparently, and they couldn't get enough of the stuff.

After he told us about his predicament he was apologetic and gave us both a very nice haircut. He quickly ushered us out of his shop when he had finished and we happily went on our way. Soon afterwards we saw a large group of the Russian sailors. They were enormous, and very smart in their navy blue uniforms, but the most striking thing about their appearance was their perfectly styled, greased back hair!

CHAPTER 22
THE FAIRER SEX

It was around this time I started to get interested in girls. Every Sunday we teenagers would all get dressed up in our Sunday best and head down to Ravenscourt Park. In my case that meant a sharp suit, straw boater and a cane with a silver handle. They were all the rage and all of my friends carried them. I looked very dapper and was confident I would be able to find a girl to talk to, despite the fact that I was on the short side at 4'11". I didn't really start growing until I left for France during World War 1. The girls seemed to prefer taller suitors, but I was a determined and confident lad and never gave up hope. There were always throngs of us in the park, trying to pluck up the courage to engage a girl in conversation. The idea was that once you got talking to a young lady, you would ask her if you could walk her back to her house. Back then it was heavenly when a girl agreed to let you walk home with her. The walk itself was often punctuated by embarrassing silences and we spent a lot of time talking about the weather, but it was all a lot of fun. Some girls were not content for their afternoon to be over once someone had walked them home, and would end up returning to the park again for another chance to be walked home! They might spend the entire afternoon doing this. I soon got wise and on the rare occasions that I got to walk someone home I would hang around their house afterwards to make sure she didn't come back out again. Sometimes however I might walk past someone in the park half an hour later and think to myself, 'She looks awfully familiar'. It was quite a game, and a fun one to play.

☙❧

WHEN I WAS EIGHTEEN YEARS OLD I BEGAN COURTING A young lady by the name of Elsie Carter. I met her through mutual friends and we talked of getting engaged. I think that would have happened if it hadn't been for the war. She was about the same age as me and worked as a nanny, taking care of a little child in a nearby home, although originally she was from Wiltshire.

I would bring her to my house quite frequently to get to know my parents. When I left for France she did her patriotic duty by going to work in a munitions factory in Shepherd's Bush, quite near to where my family lived, and my mother invited her to go and live with them in their spare bedroom to make her life a little easier. I wrote to her from France an awful lot, and sometimes she would reply and tell me about her new job and what it was like living with my family. All of a sudden the letters stopped coming, and I heard from my mother and sisters that she had been seen stepping out with other men and that on one occasion she didn't come home at all at night. I was heartbroken. It was a very sad end to our relationship and

I just didn't know what to do. My mother got into many arguments with her about her unreasonable behaviour, and I really wanted to talk to her about it, to get her side of the story, but none of our letters were private and it was difficult to write about your feelings, knowing that every word would be read by my army officers. I wrote and told her that I wanted her to stay at my parents' house and that I would try and get home for leave as soon as I possibly could and we would finally get engaged. She didn't answer my letter and of course I felt betrayed, but I think a lot of other soldiers had a similar experience. It was so difficult to try and maintain a relationship from overseas and under the circumstances I couldn't really blame her for meeting someone else. She eventually moved out of my parents' house.

After the war, when I was living back in Hammersmith, Elsie's sister Winnie came knocking at my door one day. She told me that Elsie wanted to meet up with me round the corner of my street, if I would like to come and see her and maybe carry on romantically where we had left off. I said, "No thank you!" I was over her by then and knew what kind of life she had been living and didn't want to see her again. The way she had treated me, I think I was better off without her.

CHAPTER 23

BILLIARD HUSTLER

Nowadays I love to watch snooker on the television, but back in my youth I used to play billiards. I learnt the game when I was part of my local church's Bible club. Our instructor taught us the importance of stance and tactics and I soon discovered I was reasonably talented at the game. My best break was fifty, which is a pretty good score and it became obvious to me that I could maybe make a little money on the side from this talent. I would play against friends and other members of the local Temperance Club. We played by the rule that the loser paid for the table, which cost a shilling an hour. Due to my increasing prowess it was rare that I ever had to pay and I even made a bob or two from cheeky side bets. Soon afterwards, I had a chance to shine in the billiard limelight, when I was picked to play in an annual high-profile tournament against the Hammersmith Constitutional Club. I would be representing my local Athenium Club. All sorts of games were included in the tournament, including cribbage, snooker, and billiards.

At the end of the day I dashed from work to the very

posh club and found I was the last player to arrive and I was keeping everyone waiting. The audience was crammed in tightly and page boys in little suits were serving drinks. Then I discovered the nerve-wracking news that my opponent was none other than the former English Amateur Champion. I managed to keep myself together and started with a break of forty to put him under pressure. He soon put me back in my place though and wiped the floor with me, despite my efforts. I spent most of the game sitting down, while he charged ahead gaining more and more points! However, I did enjoy playing in front of a large crowd.

MORE RECENTLY I PLAYED A GAME OF SNOOKER AT A local day centre for the elderly, which I was visiting. My opponent broke well and then I realised I couldn't see the tip of my cue, even though it was right in front of me! Getting old does terrible things to one's eyesight! Luckily my opponent was equally hampered and we played for twenty minutes without either of us potting a ball! We were both laughing so hard as the balls we aimed for the middle pockets ended up in the corners of the table, so we decided to call it a tie and end the game.

CHAPTER 24
STREET ENTERTAINMENT

A round 1911, I took over half a shop in King Street, across the road from my father's shop. Often when I closed up the shop after a long day's work I would stroll back home along Ravenscourt Avenue and watch the street entertainers who gathered there daily. It was always a fun time on a summer's evening and my good friend Con Ralph would often meet me after work and we would watch the entertainers and sometimes go to the pub for a quick pint of beer. Con worked for Rossercll and Rosserell, Engineers, in their offices. He would pass my shoe repair shop on his way to and from his office and would often come in to see me. As I have said before, I love theatre and any type of live entertainment so I looked forward to these occasions. There would be all kinds of different acts to enjoy, dancers and singers and someone with the traditional barrel organ. There was also a regular act involving budgerigars sitting on a table. Some of them were dressed up in little coats and one of them had been trained to fire a tiny cannon. The showman always showed the audience how he had trained the birds to perform each trick afterwards, which I found really interesting.

Another regular act that we often encountered was a married couple who put on a mind-reading act. The man would ask a few select people from the crowd of those gathered to watch him, to give him a personal item such as a piece of jewelry or some other item. The woman would then guess what he was holding up. We would all be totally amazed when she was able to correctly guess what he had in his hand and I could never work out what their trick was. I can only guess they must have had a prearranged list of items, or the blindfold was thin, or perhaps he used a code word to tell her what he was holding. Anyway they kept us thoroughly entertained and always received a round of enthusiastic applause.

Con and I would love to stop and watch the escapologist who called himself 'The Second Houdini'. He would be dressed in only a small vest and pants and would restrain himself with multiple chains and padlocks, before trying to escape. On one evening we watched the escapologist get himself securely chained up at around 8.00 p.m. and then left him to it while we went off to the local pub to enjoy a couple of pints of beer. When we left at around 10.00 p.m. and began walking homewards we were surprised to see our local Houdini still where we had left him, desperately trying in vain to escape his chains! He saw us and immediately called over to us to come and help him. The poor man sounded quite frantic, he was writhing around in the dust of the street. There was nobody else around so of course we had to try and come to his aid. He said there was a key under the seat but after much searching we were unfortunately unable to locate it. There wasn't much we could do and it was starting to get chilly and we were really starting to wonder how we could help him. Luckily the local policeman came along, so we left the trapped escapologist in his capable hands and walked the rest of the way home. After that night we never saw the Second Houdini again. Perhaps he went to another part of London to perform or he may have just had enough of his act after that embarrassing evening on Ravenscourt Avenue.

※

CON INVITED ME FOR CHRISTMAS AT HIS HOME AT Berestede Gardens where I played draughts with him, his brother George and their father, Jack Ralph, who were considered experts. Well, would you credit it? I managed to beat all of them, much to their annoyance! This was also when I met Con's sister, Alice, for the first time, who much later became my beloved wife.

※

BY 1913 MY FATHER'S HEALTH WAS SUCH THAT I HAD TO close my little shop and completely take over his shop in Thomas Place, with some help from a family friend, Billy Williams, who we called 'Old Bill'. When the First World War broke out I was allowed, by tribunal, to defer joining up to fight for six months due to my father's illness and the need for me to run the family business.

CHAPTER 25

MY FIRST CAR

Buying my first car was a sort of rite of passage; something you never forget - like your first kiss, starting a new school or your first job. Mine was a two seater De Dion-Bouton, which I bought in 1912 and I look back on it with enormous fondness. It was a lovely little French car of which I was very proud. I bought it so that I could occasionally take my disabled father out on day trips. I only paid £18 for it and I was very proud of the fact that the asking price was £20 but I had managed to knock it down and get myself a bargain! Two pounds was a great deal of money back in those days.

Petrol was fairly cheap at 6d per gallon and you didn't yet need a license to be able to drive on the roads. There weren't too many vehicles out and about, so you learnt to drive by driving, there was no need for any lessons.

I loved driving my car and I didn't even mind the laborious task of winding the crank handle every morning to start the engine. It would come to life with a 'pop, pop, pop'. I used to say that its solid rubber tyres were perfect for driving up the kerbs! But the solid tyres and lack of comfortable suspension made it quite a bone shaker. I had to sell my lovely little car in 1915, just three years after buying her, when I joined up to fight. A mechanic friend of mine who had let me store it under the railway arches at Stamford Brook Station gave me £10 for it - but not to drive it. He only wanted to use the engine in a motorboat he was building!

PART IV
THE FIRST WORLD WAR

CHAPTER 26
JOINING UP

My family moved house on July 27th, 1914, from Goldhawk Road to Dorville Road, the day after my sister May married my friend Will Price. Soon afterwards, the First World War broke out. I was twenty, and desperately wanted to join up right away, but with my dad's illness, the family couldn't have managed at home if I left, so I stayed behind to help with running the shoe repair shop, albeit begrudgingly.

Most of the people I spoke to seemed to think that the war would be very short, but when it continued into 1915, I was determined to do my part. I talked it over with the rest of my family and we decided that my second oldest sister, Nelly, would stop working for the electric lamp company, Osrams at Brook Green, and take over managing the family business so that I could serve my country.

So along with my two friends from Hammersmith, Ernest Boatwright and George Grieg, I went off eagerly to the Shepherd's Bush army office to join up. The three of us were given the choice of three regiments. We could join the Engineers, Transport, or the Sherwood Foresters.

Having always been fascinated by the stories of Robin Hood and his Merry Men, I couldn't help but pick the 7th Battalion Sherwood Foresters Regiment, known as the Robin Hood Rifles. We were signified by the black buttons on our tunics, the other battalions had the more usual gold buttons.

CHAPTER 27

TRAINING

We were told to go to Nottingham and report to the Drill Hall on Derby Road, and then we would be billeted out with local families from there. Every morning we had to report on parade at 9 o'clock. There was a lot of training in Sherwood Forest, which was just as fantastic a place as I had imagined from reading Robin Hood. We did our route marches through the forest and I soon became pretty accurate with a rifle, which led to me being selected for sniper training. The Sherwood Foresters Regiment was different to most other regiments, in that they trained the same men to be a sniper, scout and observer, where other regiments trained different men for each of those roles.

I encountered my first experience of the carnage of war during a training exercise in Fovant, at the foot of Salisbury Downs (now known as Salisbury Plain). We Sherwood Foresters were being taught the basics of the Mills hand grenade which would be issued to us when we arrived at the battlefields of France. We were all expected to use one of the grenades in preparation for the inevitable situation during a battle when we would have to use one for real. It seemed pretty straight forward, but we were split off into small groups and assigned to a corporal who would show us the procedure for using the devices. Once we were confident we understood the process, we were to go into a trench which had been divided into a number of bays. Our corporal demonstrated how to pull out the pin and told us how important it was that we wait for no more than a couple of seconds before throwing the grenade as hard as possible at our target. The grenades were bigger and heavier than I was expecting and had forty-eight different pieces which would splinter upon detonation, causing devastation to anything that happened to be in the way.

One of the groups being instructed was made up of people from London and Newcastle, including the battalion postman. Yes, even the postman had to be prepared in case he had to deal with a grenade. One of their number wasn't paying enough attention to the training and unfortunately thought he was being handed the grenade by his instructor. However, the instructor was not quite ready to hand it over to him, so when the poor chap went to take it from his hand, he only managed to pull the pin, with the grenade falling to the ground. The grenade rolled away from the men in the bay and in the confusion and panic no one was able to retrieve it before the thing exploded with a large flash of light and a tremendously loud noise, which left us all with no hearing for a short while. They didn't stand a chance. All five of them were killed instantly. It was an awful tragedy and affected our morale pretty badly, happening so early in our military careers. You don't expect to lose your mates before even reaching the battlefield, after all. The postman had been a father of five children, so we all put together a collection for his family in Nottingham. We were certainly shown that day that you can never be off your guard when dealing with such powerful weapons. I think it was only at that point that we all realised what a deadly business we were involved in.

Jack Rogers in his Sherwood Foresters Battalion uniform.

CHAPTER 28
OFF TO FRANCE

By the summer of 1915, we had completed our training and found ourselves full of high spirits and excitement en route for France.

We took a train to Folkestone, from where we caught the ferry across to Boulogne. I had never seen the sea, or been aboard a boat and I'm pretty certain the others were equally inexperienced. To us it was all an adventure. In Boulogne we got on double decker buses which drove us directly up to the front.

I don't know what we were expecting. I think we all had our own ideas about what we were heading into, but we were unprepared for the driving, soaking rain,. It turned the dirt into ever present mud and made everything brown wherever you looked. It was terrifying, approaching the front with all the flashes from explosions making the sky light up. Then there was the overpowering noise... It's truly impossible to describe how horrendous the noise was - I lost my hearing in my left ear, completely, and have been partially deaf ever since from the constant noise of guns, always the noise... and the death.

The officers were aware that we needed to take a break from the trenches every so often, and the constant battering we were taking. So sometimes we were lucky enough to get called back from the front lines for a rest period. It was a welcome boost to our morale. We were usually in the trenches for three days each week and then drawn back for a period of rest. They would take small groups of us away from the front and we would often stop at the large farmhouses, which the British Army had commandeered, for a good wash and brush up. We could also replace any kit we needed to and have a few well-earned, home cooked warm meals. The conditions in the trenches were too cramped for us to take a proper bath or even a shower, so it was very relaxing to be able to finally do so.

In the grounds of the farmhouses there would usually be tented villages. The tents would have witty signs on them such as 'This Way To Chat Farm: Eggs For Sale'. I think 'Chat' came from the French word for lice, and men coming out of the trenches were literally lousy. On Sunday mornings, while sitting outside their tents in these camps, relaxing soldiers would stretch out their clothes in front of them, picking the little parasites off their clothes and using candles to burn along the seams of their uniforms to kill off the lice.

On one occasion about eight of us were taken away from the front by Lieutenant Robinson, our Lieu-tenant. We worked together in four pairs and I was with Lincoln-born Charlie Shaw. We had all been trained as snipers, scouts and observers, so we needed to be extremely observant. This gave the officers flexibility when choosing who to assign to each job. On this particular occasion, Lieutenant Robinson was going to give us a refresher course in observing, on a sizable area not all that far from the farm where we were staying. We were told the boundaries of the 'game' we were about to play - the church to the right, the road to the left, and as far in front as we were able to see. He then gave us fifteen minutes to memorize everything we could see. We did as we were told, not realising that six extra items had been placed in our view by some of the other chaps. After the fifteen minutes were over, we were told to come away for a short while and the other chaps moved the things into different places unbeknownst to us. These items included washing hanging on a line, an old ladder up against a tree, and a dustbin. We returned to our observation post and were asked to write down in our notebooks any changes we could see.

This type of exercise was very helpful to us, as in reality we needed to observe as much intricate detail as possible; the more specifics we could pass on about the Germans' activities we saw, the more vital this information could prove. Lieutenant Robinson went through the notes we had made and said he was delighted with us as we had noticed just about every subtle change that had been made. There were even a few sneaky ones which had not escaped our attention, such as the removal of the face from the church clock, and moving the laundry to a washing line outside a different house. He was determined to keep our observation skills sharp and we appreciated his care and commitment to helping us get through those terrifying, testing times.

Soon enough, we had to return to the constant bombardment of the trenches, and indeed, the lice. The food was also not up to that which had been made for us at the farmhouse. When we went into the trenches our food was emergency rations which we took in with us in linen bags - four hard tack biscuits and some bully beef. This was cooked, preserved corned beef, presented in jelly, in a tin. We were advised to pierce the tin before fully opening it. If it made a hissing sound the meat had gone off. The name bully beef may have come from the picture of a Hereford bull found on the Hereford brand, which was popular. Hardtack biscuits were cheap and long-lasting crackers made from flour, water and sometimes salt. Alternative names we had for hardtack biscuits were: molar breakers, tooth dullers, worm castles, and dog biscuits, so you can imagine how appetising they were! I didn't actually mind the taste of the bully beef though. The biscuits would get crushed to dust in your haversack with all of your things banging together, so it wasn't always possible to eat them.

For dessert we would have plum jam and margarine and nothing else for three years! I was so sick of it I swore I would never again eat plum jam or margarine when the war ended. True to my promise, I never have. I much prefer strawberry jam and butter on my bread nowadays!

On days when the fighting was lighter, the cook house would try and get some hot food up to the front for us. It was best to stir it all up together quickly while it was warm and not ask what we were eating! Sometimes we would be sent a cup of tea. We would never drink more than a couple of mouthfuls, since we had to be really careful with

the water for health reasons. It was all too easy to catch
dysentery in those dirty circumstances. It meant we could
shave in the tea though, which was very welcome.

IT WASN'T ALL MISERABLE DURING THIS TIME. WE HAD A
concert party troop, '59 Divisional Concert Party'. That
was great fun and a lot of laughs. I would do impersonations and tell funny stories. We put on a show we called
'The Crumps' where I would imitate people I had seen at
the old music halls in London, George Robey, Sam Mayo,
Harry Champion and others. I would put on my old bald
wig which I had brought with me and always try to make
people laugh as much as possible. I have often been told
I'm a born entertainer and I suppose that could be right.
I've seen a lot of changes over the years in the ways people
are entertained, but the fact that people love to be made
to laugh and that laughter is able to raise your spirits in
even the worst situations has remained constant
throughout.

CHAPTER 29

THE SOMME

When we were in the trenches there was no time to think about anything except the job at hand. Since I was a sniper and had marksman skills, I was frequently out in front of the communication lines. Once inside the trenches we had mud up to our necks. Every so often along the trenches, the Royal Engineers would dig a fairly large observation post for us with a hole cut into the middle of it. They would put a steel plate into this hole which we would be able to use for observing the enemy and reporting on their movements, using the telescope and binoculars we carried in our packs and looking through the hole while staying safely inside the post. We could also use the post to fire our weapons through. We worked in pairs and would keep our post manned all day long, sending messages via a runner back to Headquarters. We took a haversack full of provisions with us. Occasionally, if a lot of activity was happening, one of us might get sent out into nomansland in camouflage gear to keep an eye on the proceedings. You would keep hidden behind a little rise, if you could, and try and take a pot shot if you felt like it. Targets barely ever appeared, though.

I would hate to think that I had killed anyone during my time as a sniper. My feeling was that our job was to observe the distant action and report back to Headquarters, in order that a plan could be drawn up, to avoid them killing us. We were also there to stop as much of the enemy's communication as possible, from reaching their own Headquarters. There were always a lot of soldiers moving up and down through their communication trenches from the front line to the second line, and we tried to put a stop to some of them.

ONE TIME WE BECAME AWARE OF A GERMAN SNIPER occasionally firing on our communications trench and our orders were to try and figure out where he was located. Three sets of us, both scouts and observers, set up watch for him from three different posts. If we saw where he was located, shooting at us, we were told to take a compass bearing so that we could compare them later that evening and see exactly where he was firing from, by using the compass bearings and drawing a line on a map. In this way we were able to pinpoint his exact location. The following morning we saw that there was a bucket there which he was undoubtedly firing through, since it had no bottom. All three of us marksmen trained our weapons on the bucket and waited for him to take the first shot. When the shot came all three of us opened fire with as many shots as possible at the bucket, in reply. With the three of us firing

I don't think he would have stood a chance at surviving, but the shots would have hit his steel helmet, so he may have been wounded rather than killed.

CHAPTER 30
BURIED ALIVE

One day we were positioned in nomansland and I got buried by debris from an explosion. I was digging a slit trench along with another sniper named Ginotti. The driving rain made us decide to dig out an overhang under which we could sit and work without getting completely soaked; I believe they were called 'funk holes', and often men would sleep in them. We kept digging away at the side of the trench, deeper and deeper, because we wanted to be able to dump our equipment bags in there. Gunfire was going off all around us and suddenly a large shell hit the mound of earth above the trench we were digging and after hearing a tremendous bang, we were aware of dirt collapsing around us. It fell on us, burying us alive. I was very fortunate in that my helmet fell over my face and saved my life, otherwise I would have suffocated, as I was buried under there for a long time. Another piece of luck was that Ginotti's legs were partially uncovered, so other soldiers could easily tell where he was and they quickly managed to pull him out. He was in quite a state, but luckily he was able to tell them where I was buried so they could get me clear as well. I was dazed and in shock, to say the least. It had been really terrifying lying under that earth, unable to move my hands or feet, but I remember I could wiggle my toes a little inside my boots. I tried to struggle and was finding it hard to breathe, but I concentrated my mind on the need to keep breathing, keep struggling so that I wouldn't start panicking. Eventually I felt the sensation of someone pulling on my boot. By the time I was completely unearthed I was gasping for breath, but somehow I had managed to survive the terrifying ordeal - thanks to the small amount of air trapped inside my helmet. I was losing consciousness and didn't know where I was so they kept me there while they administered some first aid and until I was somewhat recovered. We weren't able to see any doctors though under the circumstances we were in. We just had to go straight back in the line. After that experience I became even more fearful than I had been before. You felt very exposed in the muddy trenches, with water sloshing up to your knees, and no shelter to protect you. I preferred not to dig a hole for myself to shelter in after the experience with Ginotti and instead used my mackintosh cape over my head for shelter. I haven't been keen on enclosed spaces since that time - but I wouldn't exactly call it claustrophobia.

CHAPTER 31

CAUGHT SHORT

On another occasion my pal, Charlie Shaw, and I were on the observation post together as usual one morning; he was using the telescope and I was using the binoculars. We were on a sniping mission in nomansland in an area where there was a reasonably large stretch of land between the German Front line and our position. The Germans were located on a slight ridge. You can imagine our surprise when we observed two German soldiers casually walking down the slope in front of their lines carrying shovels, bold as brass! We watched them begin to dig a large hole down into the side of the ridge and then after quite a while, when a fairly large pile of earth had mounted up at the side of their hole, they went back and fetched a wooden box which we were able to see had a hole in the middle of it. They pressed it into their hole and we realised they had been digging an outdoor latrine, right there on the side of the hill, in plain sight. Charlie couldn't believe his eyes, "Surely no one will use it!" he exclaimed. I told him we would have to wait and see, and sure enough it wasn't long before we observed another soldier appearing and beginning to pull down his trousers! He must have thought he was safely out of our range, as he even had the nerve to pull out a newspaper and begin reading it! We decided to give him a fright and have a bit of a laugh at his expense, so we figured out that he was about a mile away and Charlie, who was the better marksman, sent a bullet flying into the makeshift open air toilet, aiming the potshot, not for the soldier, but to narrowly miss him while he sat there with his trousers around his ankles. You never saw anyone move as quickly as he did then, shooting up and running over the ridge, then ducking for cover! He didn't even bother to pull up his trousers, such was his hurry!

I HAD A VERY LUCKY ESCAPE ONE TIME, WHEN I WAS crouched in a frontline trench with my mate, Jim James. We were repelling a German raiding party and suddenly a tater masher (we called the German grenades that name because of their shape) landed right between us! It was only a yard from either of us. I have always been blessed with good luck and couldn't believe my fortune when it blasted in the other direction. Tragically, that meant it was headed towards poor Jim. He was in an awful state, with half of his face torn off, it was horrifying. I didn't escape unscathed - a tiny piece of the device embedded itself in the back of my neck. I still feel it nowadays, when I comb my hair. It reminds me of just how lucky I am and how close I came to not surviving past my mid-twenties.

CHAPTER 32
MALAKOFF FARM

A nother close shave caused us to run for our lives! Our officers had heard from a couple of German prisoners that there was a place nearby called Malakoff Farm. It was supposedly just behind the German trenches, and Command thought there might be a large machine gun post there which would be catastrophic for our side when we had to advance.

We had no knowledge of how well defended it was, so Lieutenant Robinson was asked to take two or three of his men and get as close as possible to Malakoff Farm to observe the situation. He chose me, Charlie Shaw and Frank Richards. We removed all traces of identification and blackened our faces to avoid detection. The four of us set off from a post, using a prismatic compass to help us find our way. These were navigation instruments which used a magnetic needle and a prism to enable more accurate calculations. The sentry on the post through which we left gave us a password so that we would be able to regain access on our return from nomansland. They knew exactly when we left and when to expect us back. We had wire cutters with us, which we soon found we needed, as there was a lot of loose wire on our route. After cutting through and bending back the wire we were able to gain access to the German trench, which was completely quiet and empty at that time of night. We climbed out of the trench on its other side and continued on towards the second line of trenches, behind which we understood Malakoff Farm was located.

Frank, Lieutenant Robinson and I followed Charlie down into the second trench, which was also very quiet, and again we climbed out the opposite side and continued on our way to our destination. We began to hear a lot of noise and conversation, so we stopped and listened and were able to ascertain that a large number of soldiers were present at the farm, which was all the information we needed.

All of a sudden a light came on, illuminating our position. We realised we must have been spotted, or heard somehow by the men we had been listening to. Robinson then told us to get back across the open land to our own trench, any way we could. So we ran at top speed back to the last German trench we had crossed, then across the open land and back to the first trench we had encountered on our way to Malakoff Farm. At this point Lieutenant Robinson had lost his glasses and hat and was unable to see anything at all in the dark. He was scrambling around looking for them in the dank, muddy trench. Charlie and I had to take hold of him between us and help him along as fast as possible, following, as best we could, the way Frank had gone. As we frantically climbed out of the trench we realised Frank was now missing. Where could he be? He eventually appeared, having taken a wrong turn and we quickly helped him up out of the trench. Then we were very lucky to find the place where we had cut through the wire earlier and continued running for our lives back over nomansland towards the safety of our own trench. We had to stop and rest halfway there and figure out where the post was that we needed to return to. If we had gone to the wrong post and given our password to the wrong sentry, it was likely they would have shot at us. Not knowing about our mission and just seeing unknown men coming out of the dark like that, they would have assumed the worst, that we were the enemy. We managed to find the correct place, thank goodness, and when we gave the password and were allowed into our trench the relief washed over me. I was so glad to have made it safely back from that heart-pounding little adventure!

CHAPTER 33

THE EASTER RISING

The Sherwood Foresters Regiment had been shot up pretty badly during the conflict of the Somme. A lot of men lost their lives and those of us remaining were brought back to Nottingham for some well-earned rest and so that the officers could replenish our numbers. On Easter Monday, 1916, we were ordered to go to Heaton Park in Manchester. Despite having hardly recovered from our battered mental and physical state, our next move saw us bound for Dublin, Ireland, sent over to quell the Easter riots, more lately referred to as the Easter Rising.

The Irish rebels wanted to gain independence from British occupation in Ireland and the Rising was launched by Irish Republicans. They were hoping to establish an independent Irish Republic while the United Kingdom was distracted by fighting the First World War. After our time in France we were barely ready for more combat, but we were closest to the action and had not sustained such bad losses as some of the other available regiments, who had returned from France having lost even more soldiers than we had.

About 800 of us were sent over to Dublin and, since I was a marksman, I was sent out in the reconnaissance party, who traveled first, embarking on our journey across the Irish Sea one night from Holyhead in North Wales. I remember it being a very rough crossing. We were riding on a cattle boat and the poor animals below decks were extremely distressed. Two of us at a time were on guard at the front of the boat with our bayonets fixed and ready. Our boat had to keep changing direction because they were scared there might be German submarines hiding in the water, especially as we approached Ireland. Heaven alone knows what they thought we could have done with bayonets against a submarine!

Finally we arrived, sailing up the River Liffey, and found ourselves stationed at a tented encampment in Phoenix Park. This would later be made into wooden huts, but to begin with we just had tents to live in.

The rebel soldiers had taken over a large number of the important city buildings, including the main post office and the Jacobs Biscuit Factory, from where we were frequently shot at by their snipers. It was very dangerous; at least in France we had known who our enemy was. Ireland was dreadful, women and children would spit at us and shout names as we went by. Snipers often took potshots at us. We needed to remain alert at all times. I was shot at on several occasions, but was always fortunate to be near a doorway or some other type of cover which I could scramble into to save me from getting hit. I suppose Lady Luck must have been looking out for me.

The remainder of our men had to be billeted in Galway Bay, in the Naze barracks of the Royal Dublin Fusiliers.

Staying any closer to town would have been too dangerous. I remember some of the dreadful things that happened. We were ordered not to go out in groups of less than three for our own safety, and we were to always keep our bayonets fixed and at the ready. We were in danger of being lynched.

One day we were marching down Sackville Street in Dublin and the rebel fighters opened up on us with machine guns. At that time the British Army did not own any machine guns, but the Irish rebels had managed to bring some over from Germany, thanks to the help of Sir Roger Casement. He was later executed by the British, for being a German spy.

One of our duties was to man patrols on the bridges which led into the city. We had to have our wits about us during these patrols, as the Irish got up to many tricks. One time I was on duty at Ballsbridge, and an apparently distraught pregnant woman approached, moaning and crying that her time to give birth had come and that we had to let her through the barricade at our checkpoint so she could get some medical aid. By that time we had got used to the rebel soldiers' tricks and called an officer, who summoned our own doctor. We had been ordered not to let any unauthorised people through the barricade. Thank goodness we had the forethought to do that, because it turned out she had bags of ammunition inside her jumper, tied around her belly, which she was trying to smuggle through to the rebels.

They called us the 'Black Button Bastards' because of the black buttons on our uniforms. They also called us a lot of other names which I won't repeat here. We stayed in Dublin for four months and I have never been so glad to see the back of a place as I was back then!

CHAPTER 34
PASSCHENDAELE: THE THIRD BATTLE OF YPRES

In 1916, when I left the battlefields of France I never thought I would want to return, but I was so pleased to be leaving Ireland, it was a relief to go back.

The Third Battle of Ypres, as Passchendaele is officially known, began on July 31 1917 in Flanders, Belgium and was as muddy as they come. Field Marshal Sir Douglas Haig had decided that a long-range strategy was the way to win. The town of Passchendaele itself was a small Belgian village, located on a ridge near Ypres, which we troops pronounced 'Whypers'. There had already been a bombardment of over four million shells and the next step was to take the Passchendaele ridge. Hopefully, this would then be followed by us taking the railway which ran from Ostend to Courtral and then after that to Bruges. Bruges was an important target for us because it was linked via canals to Oostend and Zeebrugge, where the German U-boat bases were situated.

We knew a big plan was afoot, because there had been heavy artillery bombardment for a couple of days. Everyone was brought forward and we were preparing for the great push against the Germans through Vimy Ridge. We frequently had to use the Menin Road as our main thoroughfare, which was a most unpleasant and muddy experience.

We worked as a mobile unit during this time of preparation, relieving others whenever we were needed. The Menin Road consisted of a six-feet wide section of duckboard, surrounded on all sides by deep shell holes which were often full of rainwater. Everywhere you looked there was only mud, shell holes and debris. These rain-filled shell holes were hazards which could almost drown a man, they were so deep! Mostly we moved at night in order that our movements were hidden to the Germans occupying the Passchendaele area. However; the pitch black darkness made for a torturous trip. The only illumination we had was from the shells exploding in the background. We would pass messages back along our lines to let each other know where the worst hazards were as we walked along, sometimes taking an hour to get to our destination. A whisper came from up ahead,

"Shell hole on your right - and it's a big one!"

Then there was a reply from one of our number, an Irishman by the name of Dormer who we had nicknamed 'Daisy' after a music hall act of the time, called Daisy Dormer:

"It's not on the right , because I'm in it!"

With that we all started to scrabble around to save him. The muddy puddle reached up to his neck and we had a struggle to haul him out. The cold, muddy water was pulling at him, and his pack full of equipment was heavy. We eventually managed to get him out and balance him on the edge of the duckboard. It emphasised to us the care we needed to take not to step off the boards along our perilous route. Often we found that some of the messages coming back to us were getting distorted, like in the children's whispering game. One time I heard someone say that a message had been supposed to be "The enemy is shelling the ridges. Send reinforcements." The message received was instead "Henry is selling his breeches, send three and fourpence!" This could have just been one of our jokes, however. We tried to make light of things as much as possible. I heard another story of a group going along the road when they encountered a man up to his shoulders in a water-filled shell hole. The man asked them to be careful not to stand on his head. The soldiers replied by asking how deep it was down there. The reply came, "Well, I'm sat on a wagon and four horses!"

Joking aside, it was a serious business. Many soldiers drowned in the deep mud during this campaign, due to the relentless rain we experienced. There were also many other casualties caused by mustard gas attacks. October 1917 saw heavy losses on both sides for little gain. On 6th November the Canadian troops finally took Passchendaele and the total number of lives lost in the campaign was close to 200,000 - 85,000 German soldiers and 110,000 Allied lives lost. What a waste of human life!

During that bloody conflict every day passed pretty much the same as the previous one. There was nothing to look forward to; come Christmas time none of us felt in a jolly mood, although some of my mates did try to cheer us up with thoughts of the festive season. We were too busy dealing with waist-high mud and bullets to really feel like celebrating anyone's birthdays or Christmas.

WAITING TO GO OVER THE TOP WAS A TERRIBLE, GUT-
wrenching feeling. We had no idea what we would face,
but knew many of us would not be coming back alive. You
never knew if one of the hail of bullets and shrapnel might
be coming for you. The Germans were ready for us
because of the previous bombardment. Many of their
machine gun nests were unaffected by the shelling. Trying
to climb the steep ridge in the face of machine gun fire
was almost impossible. As I struggled along I heard a bang
and felt a terrific pain in my left knee. It was excruciating.
I had been hit by flying shrapnel and was bleeding quite
badly. I tied some cloth around to stop the flow and luckily
was taken away back to the trenches on a stretcher. My
knee needed thirty stitches, but I was fortunate in that the
bone had not been shattered. Sadly, the British army
hospitals were all full, there had been so many injuries
during that battle, which continued to rage for months. So
I was taken off to a nearby Canadian casualty clearing
station, situated in the Belgian village of Poperinge.

As I started to feel better and my leg wound improved
I asked if I could help out at the hospital. They were so
busy and overwhelmed with casualties that they readily
agreed. I hobbled around the place lending a hand wherever I could. Mostly this involved helping to prepare
bodies for post-mortem. I watched the doctors cut open
the bodies, sometimes using a tool called a trepanner to
cut open their skulls as well, as they tried to ascertain the
exact cause of death. Then I would help them sew up the
corpses to make the bodies ready for burial. I did this
grisly task for hundreds of bodies during my short period
of convalescence. It really brought home to me the sheer
scale of the killing. I've often been asked if I would like to
return to the site of the battles I took part in, but my

answer is always 'No'. I think it would bring up too many bad memories for me.

I had been planning to return home for leave over New Year but, because of my injury and hospital stay, that was no longer possible. While recuperating I was able to write a little poem for my youngest siblings, Minnie, Florrie and Fred and send it home with a photo of myself to let them know I was thinking of them. Minnie was still able to recite the poem almost seventy years later:

"Dear Min. and Flo. and Fred,
I suppose, at 10, you're all to bed.
You won't be when I come home
Because we'll play the gramophone.
I hope you all are keeping well,
Also Rose and Beat and Nell.
Give my love to Mr. Bailey,
And does he still read the 'Daily Maily'?
If, when I come home, there's a pantomime on
Then we'll all go together - from your brother, John."

There were around six of us British soldiers in the Canadian clearing station at Poperinge. The Canadians referred to us as Imperials. One day a colonel came to visit us and told us that an important visitor was coming to the village and that we ought to go and meet him. We obtained permission and dutifully walked along from the clearing station through the village to a building on the High Street called Talbot House. It looked like a working men's club and was difficult to see in the blackout, but we eventually succeeded. When I knocked at the door it was opened by a little old lady, who ushered us in and we saw an additional six or seven soldiers seated inside the dimly-lit room. We settled ourselves, wondering what this was all about and soon enough an enormously rotund, yet commanding figure entered the room, dressed in a padre's outfit. He introduced himself to us as "Clayton, Tubby for short. And if you take note of me you will see the reason why." This was the Reverend Philip Thomas Byard Clayton, an Anglican clergyman.

He squeezed his large frame past us and made his way to the front of the room. He informed us that his intention was to start an organisation called 'Lamplight' which would provide support to ex-servicemen and their families. "I've invited you chaps here tonight to help me found this organisation." We all approved of his good intentions and gladly added our signatures to his book, thus founding what would later be known as Toc H - an international Christian movement that would go on to have 1,600 branches throughout the nation. The name is an abbreviation for Talbot House, "Toc" signifying the letter T in the 'signals spelling alphabet', which was used by the British Army in World War I. The building called Talbot House which I went to in Poperinge was designated a soldiers' rest and recreation centre which aimed to promote Christianity.

After I left the army I kept an eye on how Toc H was doing over the years and was glad to know they were successful. Eighty-one years after that important meeting at Talbot House I received a letter from the Toc H director at the time, informing me that he had just been to Talbot House, which was still standing and was now a museum and tourist attraction. He had seen those original signatures in the founding book and had tracked me down. Apparently I was the only surviving founding member at that point. I am very proud to have been a part of that organisation's history.

The Canadian Clearing Station soon came into range of 'Big Bertha', the German siege howitzer gun, and had to close down for safety. Big Bertha was a fearsome weapon, with a barrel which measured seventeen inches, making it one of the largest pieces of artillery ever fielded.

CHAPTER 36

THE FINAL PUSH

S oon after the Toc H meeting, a rumour began to circulate that the Germans were planning a big push forward. We were given orders to go back to our regiments, but unfortunately I had no idea where my regiment was located at that time and no one seemed to be able to tell me. After traveling hundreds of miles all round northern France looking for my platoon, someone eventually told me that they had been posted to Italy and I should go to the transport office in Calais to await them. It turned out they had been drawn back for three weeks of divisional leave (which I had missed out on again) and were due back by the end of the week.

When they arrived I didn't recognise any of the officers. My mate, Charlie Shaw from Lincoln was there again though. I had been with him for my three years in Belgium and France and we had got into many scrapes together and had become great friends. Charlie came from a gypsy background in Lincoln and had been used to traveling around England in an old Romany-style caravan. He was a dark-haired man, on the short side, with a jovial, round face. We were both marksmen and observers and we worked together a lot. Charlie was a better shot than I was and we were given sixpence a day extra, because of his excellent accuracy. I'm not sure why we were teamed up together but I was very glad we were. We hit it off right away during our training in England and were then posted together to the Front. We were firm friends right until the time of the final great push, which the Germans were about to launch.

We were given orders sending us to the village of Mory, near Bullecourt on the Somme from where we went right up the frontline. We snipers were going to be situated in a small extra trench, or slit trench, in nomansland which was going to be dug by working parties led by six Royal Engineers, who I had to take out and show where to begin digging.

I took them along the communicating trench up to where the sentry was positioned. He gave me the password we needed. My job was to get the Engineers out to where they needed to dig a trench and then return to the same sentry. Each sentry had a different password and we were not permitted back in from nomansland without the correct password. When I went out as a scout the only aid I had was an illuminated compass, so that the enemy wouldn't be able to spot us. As scouts, we were often assigned the duty of taking raiding parties out and bringing them back. Heaven help any poor devils who lost touch with their scout.

In the trenches there was terrific tension, so much waiting. It gave you time to think about what was about to happen, which was not ideal for your nervous disposition. Despite my trepidation at having to take the Engineers out into the dangers of nomansland, I was glad to have something to concentrate on, to help dispel the tension of waiting.

Eventually, the rumour of a great German offensive being imminent, which had been gleaned from German soldiers we had captured during night raids, was proven correct. I had not been home since I had signed up to fight and amazingly I was finally granted permission to return to England on the 20th March so that I would be there for my 24th birthday the following day. I had been so certain that I would be able to make it home to celebrate my birthday, and had written to my mother to tell her the exciting news, and that she needn't bother to send me a parcel at the front. However, once again that wasn't to be, as all leave was cancelled on the 19th March, due to the intelligence we had gathered that the Germans were planning a final offensive. I had begun to think I was not meant to get away for a break from the conflict at all. Yet again I was unable to go home and see my family. I was left to celebrate my birthday in the trench with nothing but mud. I was feeling very despondent, but unbeknownst to me much worse was yet to come.

CHAPTER 37
A NASTY BIRTHDAY SURPRISE

On my 24th birthday, March 21st, 1918, at around 5.00 a.m. a terrific noise began - the German barrage had started. You could hear nothing but gunfire. It shattered my eardrum. Eight of us, all snipers, including my mate Charlie, were in the extra trench, which had been dug by the Royal Engineers. We had been in the trench since the previous night. It was quite some way beyond our frontline and we had been given orders to keep it defended at all costs.

Suddenly the Germans started pouring out from their trenches. As German soldiers were shot down they were replaced by others. They advanced towards our front by hiding in small pockets, which they had weakened by constant bombing, not in a straight line as we had expected. They were shelling heavily to the left and right of us, but somehow, miraculously, not on us. Waves of German soldiers flowed past us, just yards in front of us we could see a group of fifty soldiers and another group the same distance behind us, but luckily they didn't come anywhere near us, as we hid, terrified, in our trench, watching them. The British soldiers were in full retreat and from our slit in the ground, all we could see was the backs of the German soldiers, as they continued forging ahead.

We stayed in our trench like that, surrounded by all of our equipment and everything we owned. We had expected to be in the thick of the fighting and instead there we were hiding in a small trench. At around 11 a.m, a group of Prussian soldiers appeared, part of the 'mopping up' party sent to finish off or round up any survivors who had been missed the first time the soldiers went through. They threw some 'tater mashers' (hand grenades) into the trench, which luckily missed me, and then came rushing down into our trench. By some good fortune, neither Charlie nor I were killed. We decided we had no choice but to put our hands up and surrender under the circumstances. By now, it was 11.30 a.m. and we had managed to hold the trench since 5.00 a.m. We were terrified and completely exhausted from the adrenaline and extreme emotion. Frank Richards had been hit by a piece of tin between his neck and shoulders and he was bleeding and holding his head.

One of the Prussian Guards was a big, fierce-looking man with a moustache. He jumped into the trench next to me, with his bayonet fixed and pointed at my stomach. I was convinced my last hour had come. I was absolutely terrified. I said "Goodbye" and waited for his deadly thrust. Instead of thrusting his bayonet into me I heard him say softly, almost gently, "Zigaretten, Kamerad?" He wanted cigarettes. I took out my cigarette tin from my pocket where I carried some ready-rolled cigarettes and offered it to him. He took a few cigarettes and then pointed at my equipment and said, "Los!" We had to leave all of our possessions and equipment there on the ground and follow them out of the trench. They then walked us back to their lines. What an absolute feeling of relief that was, although we were filled with trepidation as to what would follow! We had heard about the maltreatment of prisoners of war by the Germans and had never really dared to consider what it would be like if it happened to us. We knew prisoners were often sent down coal mines and felt fearful for our future.

Two of our number, including Frank, had been hit by the tater mashers and their legs were badly wounded, so they needed help, but the Germans were patient and took their time while we dragged our fellow soldiers out of the trench and up a slope. There were prisoners to be seen in all directions being told where to go by German soldiers. A very smartly-dressed young officer asked me in perfect English where in Britain I had come from. I replied,

"London," and it turned out he had been to Birkbeck College in London until the war started. He had been made to give up college in order to fight. He then said,

"You need not worry, the fighting is finished for you. Good day to you, gentlemen."

We were left to find our own way via a sunken road strewn with dead horses and broken-down vehicles. We had no idea where we were going. We just followed the steady stream of prisoners leaving the battlefield. Finally we arrived at a massive field in which there were hundreds of other dishevelled and broken-looking prisoners. We stayed there for the night with no food or drink. The following morning we were brought a large dixie on a cart, containing some kind of tea from which they gave us a tin to drink and a slice of brown bread each . At this point they started forming us into groups and we began marching again, this time to the railway depot. I had managed to stay with Charlie until the depot, but that was the last I saw of him, Frank and any of my other pals, who by this time had become like family to me. Charlie was put on a different train to another place, while I was put on a train to Münster. It was so sad to lose sight of someone I had spent so much time with over the previous three years and I often wonder what happened to him. Having a friend like Charlie Shaw in the line, to whom I was able to talk about my family and how I felt when my heart got broken by Elsie Carter, helped me get through the bad times no end. My heart was heavy as I wondered how I would be able to cope on my own and what terrible things were in store for me next.

CHAPTER 38
PRISON CAMP

The trains which took us off to prison camp were made up of dozens of cattle trucks with blacked out windows and barely any air vents. We were brutally shoved up a set of steps, which the Germans brought for us, and pushed inside, forty to a truck. We travelled like that for two days without anything to eat or drink, with only a small grating for ventilation up in one corner of the roof. There was no lavatory, so we had to use one corner of the truck as a toilet. The lack of drainage meant that the smell was overpowering. I only had my handkerchief with which to cover my nose against the terrible reek. You had to stand and since there was no support it was best to lean against the wall if you could. If you were in the middle part, you had to lean against each other for support and everyone kept sliding to the floor and then getting themselves back up again. I didn't know anyone and had to keep leaning up against people I'd never met before. It was very awkward and we were all terrified. We had no idea how long we would be in that horrible situation together in the pitch darkness, with the awful smell and lack of space and the constant noise from the wheels as they went over the rails. It was enough to make anyone question their sanity before too long.

After two days of hellish travel, we arrived in Münster, where we were taken to a German prison camp called 'Lager 1'. There were three 'Lagers' in Münster. When we alighted from the cattle truck we were given a slice of brown bread and something they called 'coffee' to drink. It was made from acorns and in any other circumstance, it would have been distinctly unappealing, but we were desperately thirsty. Then they marched us through the town with fixed bayonets pointed at us, while the local people lined the streets staring at us, taking in our dreadful, dirty, wet, miserable, broken appearance as we passed by. I noticed many of the local people wore wooden clogs on their feet.

Once we arrived at the camp in Münster, we were ushered through a large gate into a guardroom. We went through the guardroom and out into a yard with a central grassy area surrounded by huts, which would be our sleeping quarters. In the camp there was a hut for each nationality of prisoner, Russian, Indian and Turkish to name a few. The beds inside the huts were wooden bunk beds made from chicken wire and each man had a thin blanket. Unfortunately, the blankets had been left outside the huts when we arrived and had got soaked in the rain, so that night we had to sleep on chicken wire with a wet blanket, but at least we were no longer standing in the dark cattle truck with our bones being rattled by the constant vibration and 'rackety-rack' sound of the train. We were so exhausted from our journey that I don't think anyone had trouble sleeping, despite the uncomfortable beds. We had a sergeant major in our hut and we persuaded him to represent us as our spokesperson. He took charge of us and appointed two men each day to do tasks such as fetching our daily rations from the cookhouse. They would bring back a big dixie containing the water in which the Germans had cooked their vegetables, a slice of brown bread each and some coffee made from acorns. That was all we got to eat on a daily basis. Sometimes there might be a little bit of mangel wurzel (a vegetable which grew easily in that area) left in the cooking water which we could chew on for nutrition.

THE CAMP KOMMANDANT (COMMANDER) HAD BEEN taken prisoner by the British Army earlier in the war. He had been badly wounded and had been exchanged per an agreement between the British and German armies, whereby prisoners who were too badly wounded to fight were exchanged. He was partially blind, wore very dark glasses, and hated the British with a vengeance! We British prisoners tried to keep our huts as clean as we could, while the Russians were known for being extremely dirty. They would use the corners of their huts as toilets instead of going to the latrine. As a punishment for being British, the Kommandant would make us swap huts with the Russians every so often, maybe monthly, so that we had to take over their filthy huts while they got our clean huts in return. He would also make the British prisoners get up and march in the rain on Sunday mornings, our only day off from work. He made us march and march until he got fed up of doing so, but only ever the British prisoners, mind you.

THE KOMMANDANT USED TO SMOKE LITTLE CIGARS, OR cheroots, and one time we had been marching around the square for over an hour and he had just put down his cigar on a windowsill while he went to talk to the interpreter. One of our braver number managed to get hold of the cigar, and of course the kommandant was not at all pleased to find it had gone when he came back looking for it. He looked all over the ground, but of course, to no avail. He called us "Schweinhünde" as usual and said we would have to march until it was found, or until someone owned up to taking it. No one would do that, so he made us march around for most of the day in the rain in our already weakened state.

The camp Kommandant made us all suffer. If someone appeared not to be working hard enough, or if a fight broke out amongst prisoners, the Germans would immediately hit us with shovels or whatever else they had to hand to use as a weapon. There were no rules, they could do whatever they liked to us. Some of us were hospitalised from being smashed by the shovels. These poor souls would tell the rest of us what happened through the wire that separated the hospital yard from the rest of the camp. Every so often, there would be someone who just couldn't take it anymore and would try to escape. These escapees were always found and brought back and dumped in the prison yard, which was just off to the side of the main camp area. We could see through the fence that they were usually in pretty bad shape. Often through that fence we could see prisoners being marched around the yard with a pack full of bricks or rocks on their back, bent double from its crushing weight. I don't know how long they had to keep that up for. I might have attempted to escape if I had felt stronger and fitter. We were very close to the border between Germany and Holland, but having had barely anything to eat, I felt physically unable to travel even a short distance.

CHAPTER 39

PRISON EMPLOYMENT

At first they set me to work with the 'sanitary police'. The toilets were basically a long board, placed over a ditch. Along these boards there were about fifty places to sit, and you never knew who you might be sitting next to on them. As the sanitary police, it was our job to empty the ditches. Five of us were given a type of barrel on wheels and had to empty the excrement from the latrine ditch into it. What a reek! First we stirred it all around in the ditch with a kind of long wooden oar, stirring it until it became liquid sewage. Then a bucket on a chain would be lowered down into the sewage and another man would be standing on a ladder further down. He would grab the bucket as it came back up, now full of sewage, which he would empty into the barrel. Then, when the barrel was almost full, we would trundle the barrel along to the allotment where potatoes and mangel wurzels were grown for the German soldiers to eat, and dump it there, using a tap on the side of the barrel. Then we would spread it out. I can still remember the disgusting stench it created, especially when the wind was blowing towards camp. However, it made the vegetables grow a treat.

The mangel wurzels were around two feet high and would have won a prize at a county fair under different circumstances! The camp was surrounded by double rows of wire and vegetables were grown between the two rows. The vegetables were not for the prisoners, though - only for the German soldiers. We prisoners were on sparse starvation rations as I described before. A lot of men got the runs due to their poor diet so there was always a steady stream of people heading towards the latrines when they weren't working.

❧

ANOTHER JOB WE SOMETIMES HAD WAS PLANTING THE potatoes the lucky Germans got to eat. We would carry the tiny potatoes in our shirts and follow the plough as it made a groove for us to drop them into. Sometimes when we reached the end of the groove we still had a couple of potatoes left unplanted and from time to time someone would try and conceal them in his clothing. If the Germans noticed a prisoner looking too fat they would pat him down and, of course, severe punishment would follow if any potatoes were found on an unlucky prisoner.

❧

THE GERMANS LATER DISCOVERED THAT MY TRADE before the war was shoe and boot repairs and since the camp was home to a wood shoe-making workshop, they decided to make use of my skills and put me to work in the shop. A large number of prisoners worked in teams of two in the shoe workshop, making wooden shoes like the ones I had noticed villagers wearing when we first approached the prison camp. I would set off from the hut in the morning, collect my ration of a piece of brown bread and a can of tea and then head to the workshop. I was put in a pair with a Frenchman called Roget, similar to my own name. Standing at a double bench I would use a saw to cut large pieces of wood into predetermined widths and lengths and then hand them to Roget, who would use a vice to keep them steady, while he scooped out the wood from the centre, making a foot hole. He would then shape the sides and give them to me to trim the finished product. We did this all day long. It was very tiring, but at least I was away from the stench of the latrines, which was a blessing.

Every once in a while a group of us was taken to the railway station in the town to fetch the wood from which the wooden shoes were made. We used a small hand crane to maneuver the logs onto a cart. Then two men would pull the heavy cart and another two would push it all the way back to camp.

We were very lucky that one of the prison guards took pity on us. He was a decent chap and he would take us via the back streets into a pub garden and buy each of us a beer. We would often reward him with a bar of soap received from our Red Cross packages. The Germans could not get hold of soap very easily so these bars of soap were worth their weight in gold! Whenever we gave him one he was so pleased to be able to take it home to his wife that he would happily buy eight of us a beer!

The Cobblers 'Holzschumacher' in Lager 1, Münster,
Germany. Jack is in the front row, in the centre.

CHAPTER 40

CONCERT PARTY

It wasn't all doom and gloom in the prison camp. The French and Italian prisoners put on shows to entertain the rest of us with songs, skits and even proper plays and opera. There were sets and costumes put together by prisoners and the shows were performed in a big extended hut which the prisoners built, with the permission of the German officers. The hut had a stage and chairs were brought in, just like a proper little theatre! I sang there once with a friend called Mac, all dolled up as a lady wearing a dress someone had let me borrow and with Mac wearing a dress suit; we definitely looked the part! We sang 'If You Were the Only Girl in the World and I Was the Only Boy'. One of the French prisoners took our photo while we were holding hands and performing. We must have looked quite a sight, but it helped bring a smile to some of the prisoners' faces.

Jack Rogers performing with his friend Mac during a concert party in 1918. Photo taken by a French prisoner.

A SHOW WAS PUT ON EVERY TWO WEEKS TO TRY TO KEEP up our morale. Having something entertaining and fun to look forward to did really help. I spoke to our sergeant major to see if he could get permission for us British prisoners to put on some shows as well and he did. We soon formed the British Concert Party and set to work planning what kinds of entertaining skits we could enact. Soon we were performing monthly to packed audiences, rehearsing in our hut at night, even though we really weren't that talented!

ONE DAY WHILE MAKING SHOES I ASKED ROGET IF HE might ask the French if I could do some kind of an act at one of their larger scale shows. I told him I had done a lot of entertaining at the front with the 59th Divisional Concert Party in an act I used to call 'The Crumps'. He arranged it with the producer of the French show who was quite the comedian. He was known by the nickname of 'Tonic Sol Fa', which is a phrase that describes a method of teaching music. At their shows the front three rows were always filled by the Germans, with French prisoners filling up most of the remaining seats and then a few of us British would fill up the back of the room. It was a very international affair and I was able to pick up little bits of language here and there in order to perform part of my act in different languages. I told them I would like to perform a song accompanied on the piano by an Italian prisoner I had got to know, and then a monologue called 'Spotty'. I also wanted to sing 'Henry the Eighth, I am' and a Sam Mayo song called 'A One-Man Band'. They liked all the songs, but 'Spotty' went down a treat.

Spotty

By F. Chatterton Hennequin & Phyllis Norman Parker
(1914)

Spotty was my chum, he was, a ginger-headed bloke,
An everlasting gas-bag and as stubborn as a moke.
He give us all the 'ump he did before it come to war,
By sportin' all 'is bits of French, what no one asked him for.

❦

He says to me, "Old son," he says, "you won't have 'arf a chance,
When I gets in conversation with them demerselles of France."
I says to 'im, "You close yer face," he says, "All right bong swore,
Don't 'urt yourself mong sher amy," then "so long! oh re-vore!"

❦

When we got our marching orders you can bet we wasn't slow,
A-singing, "Tipperary! It's a long, long way to go."
On the transport 'ow he swanked it, with 'is parley vooing airs,
Till I nearly knocked 'is 'ead off 'cos he said I'd 'mal de mares'.

❦

When we landed, what a beano, how them Frenchies laughed and
cried,
And I see old Spotty swelling fit to bust 'iself with pride,
He was blowin' of 'em kisses and was singing, "Vive la France,"
Till the sergeant major copped 'im, then he says, "Kel mauvay
chance!"

❦

But we didn't get no waitin', where we went nobody knows,
And it wasn't like the fighting that you see in picture shows.
We 'ad days of 'ell together, till they told us to retire,
And then Spotty's flow of language set the water carts on fire.

❦

'Im and me was very lucky, for two-thirds of us was dead,

With their greasy 'black Marias' and the shrapnel overhead.
And every time they missed us when the fire was murderous 'ot,
Old Spotty says, "Honcore! Honcore! That's French for 'Rotten
shot.'"

❧

And then at last there came the time, we got 'em on the go,
And 'im and me was fightin' at a little place called Mo (Meaux)
A-lying down together in a 'ole dug with our 'ands
For you gets it quick and sudden if you moves about or stands.

❧

We was sharing 'arf a 'fag we was. Yus! turn and turnabout,
When I felt 'im move towards me, and he ses, "Oh mate, I'm out."
'Is eyes they couldn't see me - they never will no more,
But 'is twisted mouth it whispered, "So long matey, oh re-vore!"

❧

There was no one quite the same to me, for 'im and me was pals
And if I could 'ave 'im wiv me you could keep your fancy gals.
But he's taking French in 'eaven, and it's no good feelin' sore
But Gawd knows 'ow I miss 'im, so long Spotty, oh revore!

WE ALSO USED TO GET ANYONE TOGETHER WHO HAD A bit of singing or comedic talent or a story to tell on a Sunday night in our barracks, and have what we called our 'Barrack Room Gaffe'. It was important to try and keep up morale in those dark days of hard work with barely any food to sustain us. Whenever a food parcel came through or we had a bit of tobacco the mood was definitely much lighter. I enjoyed our concert parties and our songs, but all we really wanted was to go home. We kept the entertainment going with our concert parties until the war ended.

The British Concert Party of the Münster 1
Kriegsgefangenenlager, 1918. Jack Rogers is on the front
row, 5th from the right.

THROUGH THE HARDSHIP OF THOSE EIGHT MONTHS IN
prison camp I managed to lose over two stone (28lbs) in
weight, but I am grateful I never had to work down the
mines as slave labour. The men returning from the mines
often had to go straight to hospital, they were in such bad
shape. The mines were very unpleasant places and given
the terrible amount of work they were ordered to do,
coming up from working underground on the coalface
they were broken men. The German miners were paid by
the wagon and the prisoners laboured hard, down in the
depths, for extremely long hours. Those prisoners assigned
to mine work were chosen at random by a German officer
pulling our prisoner numbers from a hat, and the following
Monday they would have to leave, unsure if it would be a

coal mine, salt mine, tin mine or lead mine. I was extremely fortunate to avoid being picked. One day my number, 267760, was drawn and I began to panic and to steel myself for the daunting and exhausting prospect of going down the mine. At the time, along with some French prisoners, we were organising a concert party after gaining special permission from the Germans. Our sergeant major was liaising with the Germans via an interpreter to arrange the special show and since I was the president of the British Concert Party he felt that I was an important part of it. If I went down the mine I would no longer be able to take part in rehearsals and would miss the performance. He managed to find a new prisoner who was a miner by trade and persuade him to volunteer in my place. I had a lucky escape again! I was very thankful to both the sergeant major and the volunteer miner, especially since I suffer somewhat from a fear of enclosed spaces following the incident where I was buried alive with Ginotti. My penchant for entertaining had saved me from a terrible experience.

CHAPTER 41

RED CROSS RELIEF

The hunger and weakness we experienced as prisoners is like nothing else I have ever had to endure in all of my long life. We were so tired all the time due to malnourishment and were unable to sit anywhere apart from the floor, with our backs up against a wall. We were too tired to stand up, but had nowhere to sit - what a predicament! We all still wore the uniforms we were wearing when captured, which were becoming ragged and worn. Even though I was a shoemaker by trade, I was barefoot until a French soldier took pity on me and gave me a pair of wooden shoes. Our skin started to hang off our bones and became very pale. You could feel all your bones, and the hunger pains were almost unbearable. They would double you up in pain every so often, so that you felt you couldn't go on any longer. We were unable to bathe, shave, or brush our teeth, we just had to try and wash ourselves down a little as best we could. I had false teeth at the time but was unable to look after them properly. I must have weighed around six or seven stone (98lbs). The hunger pains were accompanied by extreme flatulence, since we had nothing to pass, so we just passed wind all the time.

APART FROM FOOD AND DRINK WE ALSO MISSED HAVING A cigarette. Some of the French prisoners had been there since 1914 and were receiving packages with tobacco and newspapers in them. They used the newspaper to roll up their own cigarettes and we British prisoners would see them with these and feel very envious. Sometimes we would follow them in the hopes that they might throw away the end of the cigarette and we might pick them up. They always put the cigarette butt on the floor, stood on it to extinguish the flame and then returned it to their pocket, though, so we were out of luck.

EVERY SO OFTEN THE DANISH RED CROSS WERE allowed to visit us in the camp. They were there to check up on us, to ensure we were being fed and treated properly. This happened one Sunday, after I had been there for around three or four months. Seven or eight representatives of the Red Cross came to observe our condition and take down the names of any new additions to the camp. They made a list of our names and regiments and in this way my parents were eventually able to find out that I was alive, and where exactly I was. Up until that point they had simply been told by the War Office that I was missing, and had been worried sick. The Germans had not bothered to inform anyone who they had captured.

Since visitors were coming, the Germans laid on what

felt like a proper feast for us, with dishes of different kinds of potatoes and a type of semolina they called Reisgries. They even put out a menu on a chalkboard, in front of the cookhouse, which we had never seen before. Why would we need a menu when we always had the same meager food? The Red Cross representatives were not allowed to be alone with us, or ask us any questions, since the Germans were always standing watching us, with a threatening demeanour, and we didn't want to end up marching around the prison yard with a pack of bricks on our backs as punishment afterwards, but at least we were able to fill our bellies on that day.

THERE WAS A LADY I HAD KNOWN BACK IN Hammersmith by the name of Mrs Ellis, who worked at the West London Hospital. I had come to know her through collecting bits of silver paper and other bits and pieces she wanted. I had also been making surgical boots for her, for use by the hospital. My parents contacted her when they first found out I was missing, and through the Swedish Red Cross, via the list made when the Red Cross had visited us, she managed to find out where I was being held and told them I was a prisoner in Münster. She made sure my name was on the official prisoners of war list and sent me a package of two hundred Greys cigarettes. Thereafter I started to regularly receive Red Cross parcels as well, for which I was very grateful. When I received that first package containing cigarettes, I became a very popular chap, I can tell you!

The Red Cross parcels were supposed to come every two weeks, two or three parcels at a time, but none of us

got them very often. It was a tremendous relief whenever
we did receive one, though! They would consist of food or
articles of clothing and tobacco. A party of us would be
chosen by the Germans to go down to the railway station
in the town to collect the parcels with a handcart. Out of
spite, they only allowed us to pick up a certain number of
packages each time, so the majority of the Red Cross
parcels were left behind at the railway station, all piled up
along the platforms. We would drag the cart back to camp
and then everyone would get called out on parade. The
interpreter stood on the cart shouting out prisoner
numbers and names and we would go up and receive our
treasured package. These packages were what kept us alive
as they often contained food and perhaps a new pair of
boots or underclothes, a jacket and trousers, or a cap. The
food would be tins of roast beef among other types of
solid food and we were eternally grateful for everything we
received. The downside was that our bodies were no
longer used to eating solid food and we all started to break
out in nasty boils all over our skin, round our necks,
behind our knees, around our arms and legs. I once had a
really big, sore one on the back of my neck which made
me have to bow my head slightly. We had no medication to
put on them so I would dab it with tea until it broke.
Some of the poor men ended up in the hospital covered in
boils.

CHAPTER 42
THE END OF THE GREAT WAR

One day the Kommandant called us all together out onto the parade ground. He spoke to his interpreter, and we were surprised to hear the interpreter start to address us with the word 'Gentlemen'. We knew immediately that something tremendously important must have happened, and our hearts began to soar. He always referred to us as 'Schweinhünde', never 'Gentlemen'. That was how we were told that the war had come to an end. The sense of relief was incredible and almost too much to bear! You can imagine the enormous cheers that went up from all of us surviving prisoners! He couldn't possibly keep us quiet then! He told us that the war was over for us and that all we had to do was wait until a train came to evacuate us. We were expected to sit tight at the camp until the arrangements could be made. I had been in the camp at Münster for eight months and couldn't wait to see the back of the place!

The Kommandant then told us that there was a problem we needed to deal with before we left. Hundreds of our Red Cross parcels were lying accumulated in piles at the railway station, and no one knew what to do with them, there were so many. They were supposed to have all been delivered to us at the camp, but the Kommandant clearly did not think that was important. We didn't want the German soldiers to get their hands on them, so we all discussed what to do and agreed to give them to the local villagers, some of whom were so poor they had nothing but the clothes they wore. Our sergeant major took control of the operation and invited all the poorest villagers to come down to the station. They stood in a line and we gave each person a parcel as they walked past. The looks of pleasure and disbelief on their faces were amazing. It made all of us feel good. That's what I like to remember about the Great War, not the endless days of hunger pangs and exhaustion in the prison camp or the dreadful experience of the trenches, with their incessant fear, noise and mud.

❦

A FEW DAYS LATER WE TOOK A TRAIN TO ENSCHEDE IN Holland, just over the border from Germany. It was so exciting to be leaving the prison camp at last and making our way back home. I couldn't wait to see my family and home again. We arrived there in the late afternoon to a very warm welcome from the locals, who brought us all kinds of delicious food and drink. We slept on mattresses on the floor of the local village hall. We just lay down and slept right away. The mattresses felt so comfortable after our experiences with chicken wire beds in the prison camp. The following day we set off eagerly for Rotterdam with a view to catching a ship which would finally return us to our beloved England. Unfortunately the weather was not on our side; it was too foggy for the boat to leave safely, according to the captain. It was all very frustrating, of course, as all we wanted to do was to get back home as soon as possible to our loved ones who were waiting for us!

While we waited for the weather to change, 150 of us were taken by train back to Enschede and billeted to a camp named Timbertown. The camp had been built mostly out of wood by a British naval unit who had escaped capture in 1914. Four hundred sailors had been sent by Winston Churchill to land on the coast behind enemy lines, but the Germans had been waiting there for them and they had to remain interred in Timbertown, Enschede, for the rest of the war. They had certainly settled in well, despite being stranded. Some of them had Dutch wives and girlfriends. A lot of these local women came to us to ask for news of their men, and most of them had children accompanying them. Timbertown was a step up from our prison camp and we were able to settle in quite comfortably, while eagerly waiting for an improvement in the weather. All of the marines had returned home by the time we arrived, apart from one of the naval officers, who had remained behind to welcome us to the camp. He warned us that the British Army wanted us all to return to England fit and well and that we should avoid two things in order to accomplish that; the Dutch schnapps and the Dutch women. Luckily none of us had any money to indulge in either of those delicacies. We stayed in Timbertown for three days and nights before at last the weather changed and we were able to travel back to Rotterdam for our very welcome departure for England.

CHAPTER 43
RETURNING TO ENGLAND

I will never forget the steamer ship which took us home. It was named the Kronstadt and was a very welcome sight. We couldn't believe we were finally on our way back to home comforts after so long, but then we had to stop halfway to England because the fog had returned and the captain refused to go any further at night. He was scared there might be German mines in the water, since the North Sea was littered with mines following the First World War, and that it wasn't safe to proceed in darkness. So, much to our frustration, he anchored our ship until morning. What a long night that was!

Eventually dawn broke on a damp, foggy, drab morning in December 1918 and we were able to continue full steam ahead in the daylight. Finally we came safely up the River Humber and into the east coast port of Hull. I remember it very clearly, as it was my first sight of British soil in three years.

But here we were, Lady Luck had been on our side and we had survived against all odds and were finally back in

our own beloved country. Our eyes filled with tears as we
drew near to Hull. All the local ships were out to greet us
and they were all sounding their fog horns and sirens.
Everywhere you looked there was a sea of flags and lots of
bands welcoming us. There was a real ticker tape welcome,
all raucous and patriotic. We were the first prisoners of
war to return home and everyone was so happy to see us.
There were about 150 of us on the Kronstadt. The people
meeting the boat were just amazing. They were shocked to
see the sorry state of some of us, since there were a lot of
thin, drawn, lifeless-looking people among us. This was
not really surprising, when you think about what we had
endured for the previous three or four years, but still a
shocking sight for the people greeting us. When we disem-
barked at Hull we were to go straight to the railway station
to make our way to a repatriation centre in Yorkshire.
However, this was not as easy as it sounded, since the platforms at the railway station were filled with women,
hundreds of women. I've never seen anything like it! They
made it difficult for us to get away from them and into the
carriages of the waiting train. They were all showing us
photos and asking if we knew anything at all about their
loved ones. Voices were calling out to us begging for information about which regiment we had been in. One of the
men whose picture I was shown was familiar to me. He
had also been a sniper with the Sherwood Foresters. He
had been killed in action and here was his poor mother
who nobody had told yet. I couldn't bring myself to tell
her either, so I said I had no idea where he was. It was very
sad to think that for a large number of these women no
one would be returning - there would just be an imper-
sonal letter of condolence from a commanding officer.

WE TOOK THE TRAIN TO THE REPATRIATION CENTER AT Ripon in Yorkshire, where we were told to strip and take a series of showers to ensure we didn't take any unwanted lice or disease home with us. They gave us big towels to dry ourselves off with and wrap around ourselves. Then they took all our clothes we had worn over from Germany and asked us if we would prefer to wear an army uniform or civilian clothes. I opted for a smart grey suit and they kitted me out with three pairs of socks, trousers, jacket, shirt and underclothes for the train journey back to London.

Once we had been given our clothing we had to see the doctor and tell them about anything we had suffered from or were suffering from as a result of being taken prisoner. They said they were going to hold the Germans financially responsible for everything they had caused us. I should have mentioned the loss of hearing in my right ear, but I thought perhaps it might come back since I was still young. It never did, though.

AFTER BEING DEMOBBED, I WAS FINALLY ABLE TO REJOIN my family in Hammersmith almost a month after returning from Germany. It was absolutely marvelous to see them, I can tell you! My mother, youngest sisters Florrie and Minnie and young brother Freddie met me at the door and my father, a cripple by now, was sitting in his chair. I had written to my family to let them know I was on my way, so they had all gathered there waiting to see me. Everyone made a lovely fuss of me, it was so wonder-

ful! I was the second oldest of ten children and my word,
how they had all grown up during my lengthy absence,
especially my dear sisters! That was a big surprise. But a
very welcome one as there had been numerous occasions
in those terrible trenches when I had been certain I would
never see any of my family ever again. Being away from
home for a long while makes you understand just how
important your family can be. I slept right through for two
or three days straight after getting home; it was so
wonderful to be free and comfortable once again and to be
able to relax and feel safe. We had a real London New
Year's Eve party that year, I can tell you! It wasn't too
raucous or loud, but it was so lovely to see everyone after
so long. The amazing feeling of freedom was something
that didn't leave me for a long time.

I RECEIVED A LETTER FROM KING GEORGE V AND HIS
wife Queen Mary, thanking me for my service and
welcoming me back to England, which I have always treasured. The recognition that I had tried my best and that I
had been a prisoner of war was important to me. It reads:

BUCKINGHAM PALACE
1918

THE QUEEN JOINS ME IN WELCOMING YOU ON YOUR RELEASE from the miseries and hardships, which you have endured with so much patience and courage.

During these many months of trial, the early rescue of our gallant Officers and Men from the cruelties of their captivity has been uppermost in our thoughts.

We are thankful that this longed for day has arrived, and that back in the old Country you will be able once more to enjoy the happiness of a home and to see good days among those who anxiously look for your return.

GEORGE R.I.

PART V
BETWEEN THE WARS

CHAPTER 44
NORMAL LIFE RESUMES

I was grateful that I was still alive, unlike many of the unfortunate people I had got to know over the previous three years, and was happy that I was able to get back to work and have a normal routine once more. To begin with, I went back to working at my father's boot and shoe repair shop which I had left in 1915. My sister Nelly returned to working at Osram's electric light factory, but I started thinking it was time I had my own business. I had begun to court my friend Con Ralph's sister, Alice, and we soon fell in love and became engaged to be married.

One day Alice and I were out walking in Ravenscourt Park. We went to Stamford Brook Station and right opposite was a row of little shops. The middle one, 373 Goldhawk Road, was empty and I decided to take it and begin making surgical boots for hospitals. I was still in touch with Mrs Ellis after I came back from the war, and she asked me to make a particular pair of boots for one of her patients. I soon started making others and before long all the hospitals were asking me to make specialised boots for them. I was in that business for thirty-eight years.

As well as being an accomplished pianist, Alice also had a beautiful contralto singing voice. In 1920, the year before we got married, she was invited to Peel House, on Charing Cross Road to sing at a concert which was being staged by the Metropolitan Police's 'T' Division. The house was named after Sir Robert Peel, the founder of what became the modern-day police force. The occasion of the concert was the 'passing out' ceremony of the latest crop of new police officers, ready to take on their duties on London's streets. There were to be over 500 police officers at the concert including Lord Trenchard, the police force commissioner. My fiancée was invited to perform, partly owing to her lovely voice and partly because both her brothers George and Charlie Ralph were members of the police force at the time, as had their father been. They had recommended her to Lord Trenchard. She agreed to perform six songs on the condition that I could also be booked to perform my act of jokes, impressions, monologues and a few humorous songs. Lord Trenchard agreed and we were both somewhat filled with trepidation at performing in front of a large audience of dignitaries, in such a beautiful location.

On the day of the concert we approached the imposing building, walking past all the police cars and ambulances parked in the courtyard. I was to go up on stage twice, once in each half of the performance. At the time there was an in-joke amongst the police that whenever something broke, it should be taken to the local slaughterhouse, 'Harrison and Barber'. George had told me about this joke and urged me to find a way to use it in my act, since he thought the audience would find it hilarious. If ever anything went wrong on the beat, the police officers would say: "Send for Harrison and Barber." My act was going well, with everyone appearing to enjoy the jokes and impressions of famous actors from the music hall and I was very happy to be performing once again. Towards the end of my act I had a small drum which I would beat as part of a sketch I performed. My nerves must have got the better of me, as I hit the drum way too hard on this occasion and it broke. I looked out into the audience and said, "Better send for Harrison and Barber." What a response I got! The entire audience was rolling in the aisles with laughter at that little in-joke. It has to be my best ever ad-lib. At the end of the show Lord Trenchard himself came over to ask me if I was also from the police force since I obviously knew their private jokes. I explained about the family connection and he remarked, "Jolly good show," and moved on to talk to someone else. Even to this day I still think about sending for Harrison and Barber whenever something goes wrong!

❧❦❧

I WAS VERY LUCKY TO MEET ALICE, AS SHE HAD QUITE A similar sense of humour to my own, and was fairly mischievous as well. One time when we were courting I took her to a dance. We were twirling around the crowded dance floor and she kept seeing this short man with a bald head as he danced past us. All of a sudden without saying a word of warning to me, she broke away from me, reached out and slapped him on the head from behind, immediately returning to my arms and continuing dancing. The man stopped and asked, "Who just slapped my head?" but the music continued playing, while Alice was sniggering away and trying to hide her laughter. I was bemused by her outrageous behaviour and asked her, while continuing to dance, "Why did you do that?" Her answer was, "Well, I just had to slap that silly bald head!".

ALICE WOULD OFTEN WAVE TO PEOPLE IN THE STREET AS we drove along, mimicking the regal wave used by Queen Mary, acknowledging the peasants! She was quite a character! I used to dust the mantlepiece whenever she was going to come and visit me and would move the piano around so that her voice could be heard to its best advantage. There was a little rivalry between my sisters and Alice; I suppose they were a little jealous of all the attention I was giving her, when they were used to having me all to themselves. Whenever we would have a family singalong to entertain ourselves, my sister Nell would play the piano and since Alice had a beautiful voice it was only natural that she would be asked to sing. Nell seemed to think she should play the keys in a very heavy-handed way, to try and drown out poor Alice's singing! Sometimes my sisters were a little mean and used to say that Alice only owned one hat, but used different hat pins each time she wore it to make it appear like different hats. Nell, my most outspoken sister, also famously made a comment about me having to mend Alice's shoes before her wedding day, rather than her having a new pair for such a special occasion. Alice would give as good as she got, though, and on one occasion we were all at an evening of family entertainment hosted by my sisters, Minnie and Florrie, and their spouses, and on leaving, Alice observed, "What a shame that Jack is the only one in the family that has any talent." Another time during a family gathering, she announced, "Take me home now, Jack. I'm tired and cold and hungry." It was certainly difficult sometimes, playing referee and trying to keep things harmonious and balanced between the ladies in my life!

CHAPTER 45

A BACHELOR NO MORE

I married my fiancée, Dora Alice Ralph, on 25th August 1921, at St Peter's Church, Hammersmith. It was such a happy day for us, despite the fact that Alice's father, John Ralph had passed away two months before and her brother, Con (Cornelius), who was a great friend of mine and had introduced us, had also died quite suddenly of heart failure in January 1921, just two months before he was due to turn 30 years old, after an illness possibly caused by his playing football in the cold and rain. Alice's brother Charlie was angry with us for deciding to marry so soon after these sad events and even refused to come to our wedding. He thought we should postpone our wedding until six months after Con passed away, but we decided to go ahead anyway. Her other brother, George, attended with his wife and children.

Jack Rogers and Alice Ralph on their wedding day, in the back garden of Alice's home at Berestede Gardens, Hammersmith.

OUR ONLY SON WAS BORN IN DECEMBER 1923 AND WE named him John Cornelius Rogers, after Alice's brother, Cornelius John Ralph. We moved to 13 Ravenscourt Gardens in 1925 and stayed there until 1931. Alice's widowed mother lived with us, until she passed away in 1932.

Jack, Alice and their son John in Ravenscourt Park,
Hammersmith, 1924

AS I HAVE MENTIONED, ALICE WAS AN ACCOMPLISHED
pianist and also loved to sing. She also used to enjoy
watching football with me. We supported our local team,
Brentford FC, who I had supported since boyhood, and
loved to go to watch football matches live. You see all
kinds of characters at a football match. One memory I
have is of the first time I took Alice with me to watch
Brentford. It was a cup replay game, played against
Arsenal FC. We were all crammed into the football ground
and suddenly one of Brentford's players got fouled badly,
right in front of us. We all shouted for a penalty! Dear
Alice got so excited and caught up in the moment that she
jumped up and started shouting at the top of her voice at
the referee. As she shouted, something very embarrassing,
but highly amusing happened. Her false teeth shot out of
her mouth and went flying down among the hoards of

people swaying in front of us! Poor Alice immediately went chasing off after them and for a few minutes I lost sight of her in the crowd. It was very worrying to see her disappear like that, but luckily she reappeared shortly afterwards - complete once more with a mouth full of teeth!

CHAPTER 46
RADIO TIMES

Nowadays I love to listen to Classic FM on the radio. I think of it as one of my best friends. It keeps me company in the afternoons.

Back in the 1920s I had my first experience with the wireless, as we used to call it. Alice and I had a neighbour who lived upstairs from us and who had an amazing wireless set which he had assembled from electronic components all by himself. He was very technically gifted and loved putting together bits and pieces of equipment. He proudly invited me to come upstairs and see it. It was fantastic and I was very impressed by his handiwork! There was a crystal mounted in a holder which somehow was able to receive radio transmissions. You used a tool called a 'cat's whisker', which was a very thin piece of copper wire, to find the radio transmission by touching it to different parts of the crystal. Every so often we were able to hear a voice and we clearly heard the words, "Hello, this is London calling." It was the voice of Alvar Lidell, who would go on to become a famous radio announcer.

How amazing it was to be able to hear someone else transmitting entertainment into your very own room for the first time.

Of course it wasn't long before everyone had a wireless set of their own.

CHAPTER 47

CAR TROUBLE

In the late 1920s and early 1930s tramcars were to be seen in abundance. I remember the London County Council trams used to run from Chiswick High Road past the policeman on point duty at Young's Corner and up King Street towards Hammersmith Broadway. They had two decks and the upstairs was covered. The United trams used to turn left at Young's Corner and proceed down Goldhawk Road towards Shepherd's Bush. These were open on the top deck. Both these services used overhead wires, but many other tram services used an underground cable, whereby a third line of metal with a groove in it between the other lines provided the means by which they obtained the electrical power. The underground railway was beginning to expand and there were large numbers of buses - many with solid rubber tyres. Charabancs streamed down to the coast on Sundays for day trips to Brighton, Worthing, Southend and other seaside destinations. There were also many cyclists. It was still a comparative luxury to own a motor car, however, and there were few traffic signs, no motorways, no pedestrian crossings or traffic lights and no driving test.

AFTER THE FIRST WORLD WAR, ONCE MY BUSINESS WAS established and profitable, I decided I would buy myself a Singer 8 car, registration plate YV 3070, which had a solid body saloon, with solid tyres, a little horn and a spare wheel, which was attached to the wing on the side. This model had just come on the market and I was very proud to be the owner of my own transport once again, having had to sell my first car before I went away to war.

I had been reading books on how to drive, the mechanics involved, necessary maintenance and other related subjects. I had no practical experience with regard to these matters, however, and when questioned by my wife, I said, "Don't worry, I'll be perfectly able to cope." I was sure that driving was a simple matter and that one needed only to be able to identify which pedals operated the clutch, the footbrake and the accelerator and the rest was just practice. Excitement grew in the house as the day approached when a brand new Singer 8 saloon was to be delivered.

In the front of the house were two front gates, which when opened, would just be wide enough to admit the car whose dimensions had been carefully noted. I had worked hard on making a driveway which ran from the front gates along the side of the house and terminated in a large shed, which I had converted into a garage. The shed was just large enough in length and breadth to accommodate the car. However I had forgotten to consider the need to open the car doors when the car had been parked, to enable the driver to get out and there was certainly not enough room to walk round the car when it was in the garage.

The new car was delivered by a friend named Mr Williamson who was an experienced driver.

"Shall I back it into the garage?" he asked and proceeded to reverse it down the sideway and into the garage. It fitted like a glove. He was just able to squeeze out of the door on the driver's side by parking the car with the left hand side almost touching the side of the garage. He gave me some instructions, saying that the clutch was a little vicious and must be let in very carefully.

We decided that on the following Thursday, being early closing day, an afternoon ride in the car would be ideal. Alice had donned her new outfit, complete with a tightfitting hat with a floral design in the front. Granny was all dressed up in a long skirt and a tall hat with a stiff brim with a large hat pin stuck through it and our son John was wearing a dapper boy's suit with short trousers and a wide-brimmed grey flannel hat. They all sat waiting in the dining room.

"I'll just get the car out," I said.

What happened next was very amusing in retrospect. Having started the engine with my foot depressing the clutch, I had engaged first gear and then let the clutch pedal come in far too quickly. The car seemed to take a flying leap out of the garage for a distance that was about equal to its own length, then the engine stalled. This was fortunate, as the car had come to rest just before it came into contact with the side wall of the house. To get the car into the garage had not been easy and Mr. Williamson had left the steering wheel in the position he had had to place it in, in order to provide sufficient room for him to get out. I decided to put the car in reverse. Once again I started the engine and being satisfied that I had engaged reverse gear, took all the pressure off the clutch pedal. Once again the car seemed to jump - this time backwards - and came to rest in its original position exactly as it had been before. Whereupon I got out of the car, locked up the garage and went indoors.

"Let's go to the pictures!" I said. I was ready to concede defeat on that day, but not to give up entirely!

Following this defeat, Mr Williamson agreed to give me some driving lessons and for several nights in the dark, we went out to practice. After about six of these lessons I decided that it was time for a major outing. We would go on a visit to the coast on this occasion and Mr Williamson was going to come as well, driving his own car. Brighton was to be the destination and we were going to follow, keeping Mr Williamson in sight. Everything went well this time and we enjoyed a lovely day trip to Brighton and I was finally able to feel proud of my new car and newly acquired driving skills!

❄

AFTER I HAD BECOME A MUCH MORE ACCOMPLISHED driver, I was driving my brother-in-law down to Brighton for the day and a funny thing happened on the way. We were driving down a steep hill and my brother-in-law shouted,

"Look at that, Jack!"

There was a wheel bouncing past us down the hill and we found it highly amusing until we realised it was our spare wheel and it had come off of our car! Luckily it bounced over a fence and into a field nearby. The nut which had been keeping it in place had worn away, so after that day I always made sure I thoroughly checked it was safely attached before I started out!!

ANOTHER TIME I WAS DRIVING MY PARENTS AND SISTER Nell home from the south coast in the Singer 8. We had been visiting relatives in Eastleigh, Southampton, who had arranged a large family gathering. The gathering had lasted most of the day and there had been a lot of talking about old times and quite a bit of drinking as well. It had been quite a triumph to manage to get my father into the car, disabled as he was, but we eventually managed to get him into the front seat, with my mother and sister Nell in the back. As we approached Hounslow, where there used to be a fork in the road with a lovely pub called the Bedford Arms, which is now where part of Heathrow Airport is, I thought that by now my family would need to get out and stretch their legs and perhaps have a drink, which they did. I got them a drink and we all got back into the car ready to complete our journey home.

We were going along Chiswick High Road, near Hounslow, only about seven miles from our home in Hammersmith when I realised the brakes had ceased functioning. I realised I must have forgotten to take off the handbrake after the Bedford Arms and I'd been driving all this way with the handbrake getting hotter and hotter until the brakes had stopped functioning! The traffic lights were on red up ahead and I was going at about twenty-five miles per hour. I jammed my feet on the brakes but nothing happened. The lights were getting nearer at an alarming rate.

I suddenly realised what I had done wrong. Since the

handbrake had been left on, the ordinary foot brakes had overheated and no longer worked. If I took off the handbrake I knew the brakes would eventually start working again, but I was unable to slow down or stop until that happened. To my absolute relief, just a couple of yards from the traffic lights, they changed to green and we sailed on through the junction without any mishaps. I managed to keep calm and my sister and parents had no idea what was actually going on.

Following the lights, I was able to maintain the steady speed of around twenty miles per hour but there was still no way I could stop the car, and we had another set of red lights up ahead at Turnham Green Terrace. Again, right before we got there they changed to green. As I always say I am blessed with good luck, but I was sure it couldn't hold out for much longer! The third set of traffic lights came and went in much the same way. Lady Luck was certainly smiling on us that day! There was still a major junction to deal with at Young's Corner before we reached our destination. The junction was the final obstacle to deal with, but the most dangerous. It was busy and also had a busy tramline running through the middle of it. A very daunting prospect! Somehow, although I will never know exactly how we managed it, we made it through the junction without a scratch. We'd now been going non-stop for about six miles. Imagine trying to do that in London these days!

We were now only a mile from my parents' house, Dorville House. We had to cross over Paddenswick Road and there was a tram going by so I had to quickly cross the tramlines in front of the tram. I remembered that there was a slight incline nearby, and that I would be able to slow the car down on it. Finally, we turned into my

parents' road in Hammersmith. My brakes had just started
to bite a little bit once more, and with a combination of
that and driving against the kerb I was able to stop the car
a few yards past the house. When we got inside the house
my nerves were in tatters and I felt completely exhausted
as a result of all the tension. I asked my parents if I could
rest a little before driving back to my own house, because
I wanted to give the brakes a chance to cool down properly first. It took me over an hour and a cup of hot sweet
tea to eventually recover my nerves that day. Finally I went
outside and could feel that the handbrake was now cool, so
the car started and the brakes began to work as I drove
home to Isleworth. I never told my parents this story -
they remained blissfully unaware of how close we had
come to disaster!

IN THE LATE 1920S I WAS ON ANOTHER MOTORING DAY
trip with my younger brother Freddie. We were accompanying a friend of mine to Brighton for the day to enjoy
some sea air and I was following along behind his car, since
I wasn't altogether sure of the route. We made our way
there and had a lovely day on both the Palace Pier and the
West Pier, enjoying their stalls. We had a look at 'What
the Butler Saw', a popular saucy film reel you could view by
putting a coin into a kind of machine located on the pier
and then as you looked through the eyepieces you saw a
short film of a lady getting undressed down to her under-
wear, made to look as if you were a butler peeping through
a keyhole. There were a number of other attractions on
the pier as well, mostly designed to make you spend your
hard-earned money. Suddenly my friend told us he was

going to have to leave Brighton and head back to London, because his wife wasn't feeling well. He made sure I knew the way home before he left and of course I reassured him that I did, since I didn't want to give him anything else to have to worry about. So my brother Freddie and I stayed in Brighton for a few more hours and then decided to set off back home. We headed past Preston Park on our way north, and passed signs for Portsmouth and Guildford and I realised we were becoming increasingly lost. It was getting darker and neither of us could find anything we recognised from our journey there. Suddenly we rounded a bend and found a large common on either side of us. I could see some signs up ahead and slowed right down to read them. As I slowed I noticed some things in my head-lights which appeared to be dancing around on the road in front of us. Freddie and I were transfixed. We were city boys and had never seen anything like this - hundreds of little creatures bouncing about on the road as if they owned the place! Of course they were frogs, probably trying to make their way from one pond to another; there were enough for a small army of them! I had to wait for quite some time before they moved off the road and allowed us to continue on our way.

A few miles further on, we had more trouble. The car began to splutter and gave a judder before coming to a complete stop. We had managed to completely run out of petrol. We were right in the centre of Wimbledon Common in the dark and there was nothing for it but for me to set off walking with a petrol can and try and find somewhere I could fill it. I told Freddie to leave the car's headlights on so that I might have a chance of finding the car again in the darkness.

I walked for miles and eventually found a garage that

was still open and able to sell me a can of petrol. Gratefully I bought the petrol and made my way back to the car,
which took what seemed like an age, despite my hurrying
along as fast as I could. I found my brother waiting
patiently for me in the car.

It was past midnight and we still had quite a distance
to go. When we arrived back, I gratefully dropped Freddie
at home and made my way back to my own house, which I
finally reached at about 2 a.m. Our mother had been fret-
ting about our safety and had been to the police station a
few times to see if anything had been reported to them
about an accident. We were fine, of course, just very tired
and with a funny story about a few hundred frogs to tell
them the next day!

I HAD A COUPLE OF OTHER CARS AFTER THE SINGER 8.
The last car I ever owned was a Morris 10 which I
managed to keep for nearly thirty years. The Morris was
hard to drive compared to modern cars, There were only
three gears so you had to use first gear to go up any road
surface which was even slightly inclined. It was time
consuming, to say the least! To change gears you had to use
the 'double de-clutch' method which in itself is compli-
cated and takes some mastering.

IN AROUND 1930 I HAD A RUN IN WITH THE TRAFFIC
police, which I will never forget. Around that time
motoring had begun to really take off and suddenly there
were a great many more cars on the road. This had led to

an increase in the number of traffic accidents around the country, so the powers that be decided to introduce a new 'Halt' sign, as a major cause of accidents was people not stopping at stop signs and charging on through the junction. The new signs suddenly appeared overnight without any warning and caused an enormous amount of confusion and surprise amongst motorists. The following morning, which was a Sunday, the prime day for going out on a motoring trip, no one was sure how long you were supposed to stop at the signs for. It was a source of much consternation. By chance this occurrence took place in August, during my family's holiday, which that year we had taken in Devon. We found ourselves approaching a junction in Somerset, which had one of the new halt signs and there was a car stopped in front of us, obeying the new sign. It started again and drove across the junction. Now it was my turn. I slowed down, but neglected to come to a complete stop, and then slowly crawled my way across the junction, after noting that it was safe to do so. Suddenly there was a rustling noise in the bushes at the side of the road and two stern-looking policemen popped out from behind the hedgerow, shouting for me to stop the vehicle. They peered down at me in our little car and asked if I realised I had failed to stop at the halt sign. I had to agree with them that I had merely slowed down and not come to a complete stop which meant, to my embarrassment, that I had committed a traffic offence. The police officers began to fill out the required paperwork, taking note of all my details and a week later I heard from a solicitor, telling me that I would have to go back to Somerset to appear in a county court and have my case heard. By this time I was back at work in London and unable to take any more time off from my business to go back down to Somerset for what felt like a petty offence. Instead I would have to pay the £7 fine, which was a lot of money back then, but I didn't really have any choice. That weekend the authorities must have raked in thousands of pounds in fines, as unsuspecting motorists like myself up and down the country were caught unsure how to proceed in the presence of the new signs. I wonder what they spent it all on!

AROUND 1950 I HAD A NAVY BLUE MORRIS 10 WITH leather upholstery, in which I used to amuse my nephew, Jon Ralph, by driving along without using my hands, steering the car with my feet. Of course I wouldn't have done this if Alice had been in the car! She would have definitely put a stop to my fun!

I DECIDED IT WAS TIME TO STOP DRIVING IN MY seventies since it was by then more stressful than pleasurable. I was surprised at how easily I took to motorway driving, despite it being near the end of my motoring career when most motorways were built. In those days they were called open carriageways and were a pleasure to drive on. I used to drive like the clappers on them all over Britain, from Cornwall in the south west to Loch Ness up in Scotland. Maybe I should have been a racing driver!

Jack and Alice Rogers with their five-year-old son, John
Cornelius Rogers and Alice's mother, taken in Runnymede
by family friend Elsie Radley in 1928. The car is the Singer
8 Jack bought following the First World War.

CHAPTER 48
HATS OFF TO DAY TRIPS

My wife and I loved to go for day trips whenever we got the chance and we would often be accompanied by Alice's sister Grace (Lilian Grace Ralph) and her husband, Frank Egan. One time we had noticed advertisements for a special bank holiday excursion which was being run by London United Tramways and would be setting off from Shepherd's Bush Green. The destination was Hampton Court Palace, which was only about twelve miles away, but we thought it would be fun to have a day out and travel on a tram for a change. It was a special offer and fairly cheap for the time, so we bought our tickets and eagerly looked forward to the arrival of the day when our outing would take place. We imagined ourselves strolling grandly around the beautiful gardens of the Palace, which used to be home to King Henry VIII himself, and we decided we had better get all dressed up in our finery for the occasion. I wanted to look my best, so I went to Dunn's store in Hammersmith and bought myself a dashing new straw boater. I remember it cost half a crown (about twelve and a half pence) but it made me feel very posh and dapper and I felt it was well worth the expense.

When we arrived at Shepherd's Bush Green, just before 8.30 a.m., to meet the tram by which we would be traveling, there was already a fairly large number of people on board. Luckily, the two double seats at the front on the top deck were still available, which we thought would give us a wonderful view of the countryside as we embarked on our journey. We quickly sat down and made ourselves comfortable. Unfortunately, we soon realised why no one else had taken the front seats, as our tram started to trundle faster and the wind began to pick up. We didn't have much shelter from the wind blowing straight at us.

A lot of people wore straw boaters for day trips back then, but, sensibly, they used to attach them to their jackets via a thin strip of material or string to keep their hat secure in situations such as this. I had only just bought my lovely titfer ('titfer tat', cockney rhyming slang for 'hat'), so I had not yet fastened it onto anything. Of course you can imagine what happened. The tram sped up as we approached Young's Corner and a big gust of wind took hold of my hat and blew it back off down the road in the direction we had just come from! I was very proud of my new hat and there was no way I was going to just let it go, so up I jumped, quick as a flash, with a view to chasing it down. I quickly ran down the tram stairway and hopped off onto the road, which in itself was an athletic feat, let me tell you! I thought I would be able to retrieve my hat pretty easily, but the wind had other ideas, picking it up and pushing it further away from me each time. The tram driver was aware of my predicament and had slowed the tram down so that I might jump back onboard more easily, but he was only able to do this for a short while, owing to the particular stretch of road we were traveling on. Eventually, after much exertion, I managed to grab my hat and run hell for leather back towards the tram. By the time I reached it I was completely exhausted and I felt like I had been running forever. It was probably close to a mile, actually. All seventy of the other tram passengers had seen what was happening and had turned around to watch the comical spectacle. They had waved at me and cheered me on, and a massive round of applause rang out when I managed to haul myself back on board. I took a bow and made my way back to my seat at the front of the bus, where I proceeded to fall straight to sleep, as tired as I was, and missed the whole of the remaining journey. When we arrived at Hampton Court Palace I was far too tired to enjoy the gardens. Instead I found a quiet area and sat there resting until the end of the day. The events of that day certainly taught me a lesson to always attach my hat carefully, in order to avoid such a wardrobe malfunction in future.

CHAPTER 49
THE 1930S - A TIME OF FAMILY LOSS

Growing up with such a large number of siblings, and living in such close proximity to one another, we were always a very close-knit family. This close attachment continued after we all married and started families of our own. I always loved getting together with family members as often as possible. There was definitely still some rivalry between my wife Alice and my sister Nell, but on the whole we were a close bunch who thoroughly enjoyed each other's company.

Sadly, my younger brother Freddie died of pernicious anaemia in 1933, aged just twenty-six. Alice and I were still living in Ravenscourt Gardens at the time, practically next door to the Royal Masonic Hospital. Being a Freemason I had hoped to persuade my parents to allow me to exert my influence at the hospital and have Freddie admitted there so he could be properly attended to by expert doctors. My parents were convinced that their doctor was up to the job, however, and would not allow this. Their 'quack' doctor prescribed the treatment for anaemia to simply be the eating of raw liver every day and no medication.

Freddie detested eating liver and I can't imagine he ate too much of it. It soon became apparent that the liver was not helping him and that he was dying. He died some weeks later at their home in Dorville Road never having received a vital second opinion. His death had a big impact on the whole family, of course, but I was especially devastated, since I was sure if they had only listened to me, this tragedy could have been avoided. The anger and frustration I felt at my inability to persuade my parents on this matter never really left me.

My mother passed away in 1938 at the age of seventy-four, and I never really got over that loss. I was closest to her and was most similar to her in personality. We had shared our passionate love of theatre and our sense of humour and I have many fond memories of our trips to the theatre together. Her death was unexpected after only a short illness, which was treated at home. My father had been in ill health, particularly with his gout, for most of my life, so his passing, in 1939, was not such a shock to my system. He and my sister Nell had moved out of the house on Dorville Road when the Second World War was declared on September 3rd of that year. They had gone to stay in Eastcote with my sister, Beat, and her family. They were worried about living in London during the expected air raids and Eastcote was considered a safer place, as it was located on the perimeter of London. Unfortunately my father passed away just two months after moving house, at the age of seventy-six. I often wonder if the tragic loss of my mother played a role in his passing just a year after her, but I don't like to dwell on such sad times.

CHAPTER 50
PRACTICAL JOKERS

My family have always been fond of playing practical jokes on one another. After marrying Alice, I realised that she was just as much of a practical joker as I was. She even started playing a joke on me after we went to bed, when the lights were out.

She would take off her elastic stocking suspender clips and fling them at the bedroom wall. They made quite a loud 'ping' noise and I was quite taken aback. I had no idea what caused the noise I heard and Alice would say,

"There's that noise again, Jack, whatever the devil can it be?"

Being a mischievous type, she never admitted to me what was making the noise! She continued to do this every night for many months! I'm surprised she managed to keep the joke to herself and not burst out laughing!

AFTER HER DEATH I FOUND OUT FROM HER SISTER, Grace, about another trick she had played on me in the

bedroom. Grace and Alice had been shopping together and Alice couldn't stop laughing. Eventually she was able to calm down and tell Grace about a trick she had played on me the previous night. She had rigged up a brick tied to a string which was connected to the bed-frame and when I was just about to fall asleep she pulled on the string and let it go so that the brick fell to the bedroom floor. She shouted out

"Jack! What's that noise? Is there someone downstairs?"

So of course I had to get up, out of bed and go downstairs to have a look. I checked all around everywhere and found nothing amiss so I went back to bed. As soon as I started to drift off to sleep once more, Alice repeated the trick. She did this about three times in total and each time I dutifully got up and went downstairs to have a look around, finding nothing! I was very confused as to what could be making the noise, I can tell you. I'm surprised Alice was able to keep a straight face during this whole escapade. She certainly didn't give the game away.

MY SON JOHN WAS EQUALLY MISCHIEVOUS. HE HAD A cousin, Ted (Edwin Ralph) who he was very close to, they were almost like brothers. At a certain point in 1937, when John and Ted were fourteen, Ted was staying with us at our house at Harewood Road, Isleworth, while his mother was in hospital. John and Ted put their heads together to try and come up with a joke to play on me. They decided it would be very funny to set an alarm clock for the time at which I would be having my weekly bath on a Saturday evening. They then placed the set alarm clock under the bath and hid somewhere where they would be able to gleefully hear my reaction! I'm sure I probably made a loud exclamation when it went off; I can tell you it gave me a terrible fright!

CHAPTER 51

LIFE UNDER A FLIGHT PATH

Living where we did at Harewood Road, Isleworth, West London from 1933 until 1958, we were very close to what is now the world's busiest airport, now known as Heathrow, although back then it was called London Airport when it officially opened for civilian use in 1946. I remember it's beginnings as a huge empty, spare piece of land located behind a fork in the road as you drove out of London. It was on the road from Hounslow. You bore left towards Staines, right towards Colnbrook. The roads in the area were used to test out different highway surfacing techniques and materials before they were more widely used throughout the country.

There used to be a lovely pub at the fork in the two roads, the Bedford Arms, which we would stop at on our way home from our day trips down to the south coast. You could enter the pub's car park from either of the two roads and enjoy a quick half pint before embarking on the last leg of the journey. The beginnings of the aerodrome that would become today's colossus were just before the

Second World War. It was very small to start off with and used by only a few small aircraft.

Back then, aerodromes were quite a novelty and we would often leave our house on a Sunday and drive the three short miles to stand on the verandah at the control tower and watch the planes take off, circle, and land up ahead.

We read more and more in the newspapers about how Heathrow was going to be developed into a major airport. Local residents would meet up to voice their concerns about the noise level and the disruption to their daily lives which they could surely expect with such a huge development being planned right on their doorsteps. From three miles away we still found the noise of the planes deafening as they got successively bigger. They were flying so low over our house in Isleworth that if we watched them from our garden we were able to see the passengers' faces through the windows!

It got so bad that the sound would keep me awake at night and I would find myself counting planes instead of sheep to try and get to sleep. However, it didn't really help. The road traffic doubled, bringing passengers to the airport and then taking them away again and they also built new railway lines to bring in even more passengers. We felt like we were being surrounded and engulfed by all the Heathrow business. Many people in the area surrounding the airport qualified for double glazing from the council to help with soundproofing from the terrific noise of the planes. Every couple of years residents were also able to claim for a new roof from the council as the planes would cause a kind of vortex which used to rip off the tiles from the houses below the flight path.

By 1958 we could take it no more. We packed up all of

our belongings, which were a fair few, since we had lived at Harewood Road since 1933, and moved down to Sussex on the south coast of England. Finally we could enjoy the peace and quiet and lovely fresh sea air. There was not one aeroplane to be heard - what bliss! Nowadays Heathrow is more like a city with the number of people it employs and the hotels surrounding it. It's amazing to think back to the early days when we were eager to go and watch the first few planes taking off. I wonder if the little old pub survived all of the development! Somehow I doubt it.

PART VI
WORLD WAR II

CHAPTER 52
LUCKY ESCAPES IN LONDON

During the Blitz, London wasn't the safest place to live, to say the least. I was too old to enlist when war was declared in 1939, which was something of a relief, but I did want to do my bit for my country, so I spent the Second World War working as an air raid warden.

My son John bravely enlisted in the Royal Air Force in 1942, when he was nineteen. It was hard to believe that after all of the pain, suffering and senseless loss of life our country had gone through back in World War I that here we were again, once more taking part in a world war. I was sad that John had to go through such a difficult and heartbreaking experience, but also proud of him for enlisting.

As a warden, I worked with Alf Adlington, and we would share our duties, so that one of us would be on patrol, while the other one would man our little headquarters, which was a bit like a police telephone box, only smaller. Our shifts were six hours long and we had to make sure there were no chinks of light coming through anyone's curtains, since that might help the German bombers with their targeting. During my time with the ARP, the head of our area was a smallish man called Mr. Darcy who was something of a pain in the neck. He kept on telling me I wasn't patrolling our patch properly to make sure the blackout regulations were being strictly adhered to. Well, one evening I got my revenge on him for his complaints, good and proper! I was checking the homes in the area and saw one up the street with a light clearly visible. Off I went to knock purposefully at the door and who should answer but Mr. Darcy himself! I was very pleased with myself as I bellowed,

"You've got a light on there, can you put it out?"

I don't think Darcy knew what to say, he looked so flustered. He quickly went scuttling back inside to block out the lamplight.

ONE TIME WHILE WALKING HOME AT NIGHT, AFTER I had finished doing my rounds, I saw a doodlebug bomb fly over. It was a terrifying experience. The sound of the engines cut out and then I saw it go down less than a mile from the Golden Kay estate where I lived, causing total destruction. When you heard their engines cut out it was anyone's guess as to where they would fall. Again Lady Luck was on my side that night and it wasn't my turn to die. Dozens of other poor souls were not so lucky on that occasion.

ANOTHER TRAGIC EPISODE I REMEMBER FROM DURING the Second World War concerned the local picture house

near where I lived. German bombers had launched an attack on the area and the Regal Cinema was packed with film-goers at the time. Everyone was told they should either stay in the cinema or go across the road to shelter in the cellars of the Convent of the Sacred Heart, which doubled as an air raid shelter. Unfortunately the majority of people decided to go over the road to the convent rather than staying in the cinema. A bomb was dropped right on top of the convent, killing 120 and demolishing the building. It was a terrible tragedy, pretty much the worst single loss of civilian life in the capital during the war, and something I will never forget. This is one of my saddest memories of my time growing up and living in London, but on the whole I'm full of fond memories for the place. I suppose the saying is true for me: 'You can take the boy out of London, but you can't take London out of the boy.'

❧

ON ANOTHER OCCASION, I WAS WORKING IN MY SHOP IN Stamford Brook, near Hammersmith, towards the end of the war when the Germans were using deadly V2 rockets, which were silent. We used to call them UFOs. You couldn't possibly prepare for an attack of that type. You had to pray for luck and hope that it wouldn't be your business or home that got hit. All of a sudden a V2 came down a few hundred yards away from us, destroying dozens of houses and a school. All of the glass in my shop windows shattered and splinters flew at me, since I was working on the display in my shop's front windows at the time. I had put protective tape on my windows and luckily because of that I wasn't hurt by the broken shards of glass.

MY WIFE, ALICE, ALSO HAD A LUCKY ESCAPE AT OUR house. It was during an air raid and a blast from a dropped bomb's explosion catapulted a large iron bar into our house, right through the front porch. The bar ended up on top of our couch, which my wife had been sitting on just moments before! Luckily she had gone into our Morrison shelter for safety at the sound of the air raid siren. The Morrison shelters were in every London home at this point. They were like a long, steel table under which you would sit during an air raid. They were incredibly strong, thankfully, and if necessary could support the entire weight of a house. We were both extremely grateful for their existence that day!

WE SUFFERED PARTICULARLY BADLY FROM AIR RAIDS because we lived near to the Heston Aerodrome, which was a target for the German bombers, or Luftwaffe, as they were called. Our army had tried to fool the Germans into believing we were better defended against air raids than was the case, by erecting big wooden artificial anti-aircraft guns all along the Great Western Road, which would be visible to the German aircraft as they flew over-head. These were an amazing sight when they were first erected, but we soon got used to seeing them lining the main road as we went about our business. They gave us a little piece of mind, even if they were fake!

EVERYTHING SEEMED TO BE RATIONED DURING THE Second World War, and queues would form on every street. People were used to all kinds of food shortages and making do with substitutes. One time a woman we knew told us that she had seen a queue and because she was so used to queuing up for food, she just joined it, without asking what everyone was waiting for. It turned out that the long line of people was actually waiting to go into the theatre and had nothing to do with food at all. After an hour she decided to ask someone what they were queuing for and they replied:

"The Tales of Hoffman."

Her confused comment to the theatre-goer was,

"Oh, how do you cook those?"

CHAPTER 53
THE YEAR I ALMOST MISSED MY CHRISTMAS DINNER

During the war, petrol was rationed, so my poor car spent most of that time up on bricks in the garage and I travelled most places by bicycle. On Christmas Eve 1940 I was eager to get home from work on my trusty bike and spend time with my wife and son. I had just finished my rounds as an Air Raid Protection Warden. The streets were dark and virtually deserted and I was looking forward to being inside my warm cosy home. Unfortunately as I climbed the Syon Lane hill on my bike a car came from nowhere, traveling way too fast in the gloom, and crashed into me, leaving me in a heap at the side of the road. I was dazed, my shoulder seemed to be dislocated and I could feel blood pouring from my forehead. To add insult to injury, my trusty iron steed was somewhat mangled and lying in a pile nearby. I lay there helplessly for what seemed like forever, until someone eventually passed by and found me and called for an ambulance. What a stroke of luck that they happened to be passing right then and were kind enough to help me!

Later, at West Middlesex Hospital it was decided that

the gash in my head was too large for stitches, so they had to fill it with a type of plaster, after shaving the hair away from that part of my head. I had lost track of time, in my dazed frame of mind, but knew my family would be very worried about my having failed to arrive home after work, especially as it was Christmas Day the following day and I hadn't been able to get a message to them. I wanted to leave the hospital as soon as possible, but the doctors insisted that I stay there overnight. The matron told me I was not in a state to go anywhere.

I can be very stubborn and I persisted until eventually she said that if I stayed under their observation for another couple of hours she might consider setting me free. I suppose she was hoping I would fall asleep and then sleep through until the morning but I was very determined to keep awake and get back home. After two more hours of drifting in and out of sleep I asked once more if I could leave, and this time they agreed to release me as long as I returned on Boxing Day for a check up. My head was covered in bandages and I must have made quite a terrifying sight as I climbed back into the ambulance and was driven back home at last. It was only a short journey and was now approaching midnight; five hours or more had passed since I had the accident. My poor family had been beside themselves with worry. They were delighted to see me, however shocked by the bandages and my fragile state! I still have a scar on my head to commemorate that day, and every Christmas Eve I remember that dark night when I almost didn't make it home for the Christmas festivities!

CHAPTER 54
PEA SOUPER

One time in November 1941, I was returning home from working at my shop, by bicycle (I had managed to fix my trusty iron steed after the previous Christmas' accident), when all of a sudden a really thick fog descended - what they used to refer to as a 'pea souper', due to its consistency being so thick you couldn't see through it and the smog was a sickly yellow colour, somewhat similar to pea soup. I could only see about ten yards ahead, it was like a dark curtain being drawn in front of my face. A mist had been in the air all day, but nothing quite this bad. It was too dangerous to ride my bike so I jumped off and began pushing it along the eerily empty streets. It was really quiet with the fog deadening any sounds around me and I started to feel like I was the only person alive in the world. I had to use my handkerchief to cover my face for protection from the nasty smog. As I walked along I carefully peered down all of the side roads to make sure I still knew exactly where I was.

I was headed towards Youngs Corner, which was a very

busy junction back then, but on this occasion it was deserted. Every few yards I would have to stop and listen for traffic to make sure it was safe to cross the road junctions. I was walking up Chiswick High Road towards the Gunnersbury roundabout when I encountered a few cars and a lorry. The visibility was so bad that it was too dangerous for them to drive, so they had parked against the kerb and six or seven of the drivers were standing by a furniture delivery van at the head of the convoy, trying to decide what they should do and how they might reach their destinations safely. They were considering sleeping in their vehicles and continuing in the morning.

When they saw me they asked where I was headed. I replied that I was trying to get to the Great Western Road and it turned out that they were heading there as well. They asked me if I would mind walking ahead of them for a mile or so until they got to the next main junction, to help guide the way. I agreed and set off about a yard or so ahead of the first vehicle, which had its lights on to help me find my way. We were approaching the next roundabout, which led to the Great Western Road and I remembered there was a little bank on the corner and we needed to take the exit nearest to it. I managed to make out the bank's sign in the dim headlights and we continued very slowly because I didn't want us to miss the exit and be forced to go all the way around the roundabout again.

This is exactly what happened, unfortunately. I was unable to get the driver's attention in time for him to make the turn onto the exit we needed. I also realised at about this time that I was no longer sure where we were. It didn't look familiar at all, although in smogless daylight I probably would have recognised it. Just as I was about to admit to the drivers that they were going to have to negotiate the roundabout once more, a very tall policeman appeared out of the fog and came to my rescue! Luckily it was Inspector Wallace, my next door neighbour. He was out helping commuters get home safely and was certainly a godsend for us. He told me to leave it with him and concentrate on getting myself home in one piece, and he would get the convoy safely to their destination. I was relieved to say the least and made my way home, eventually arriving around 11 p.m. I was fine, if tired, after my six-hour journey, but my face was black from the smog - apart from the part which I had covered with my handkerchief. My wife told me I looked like a coal miner!

CHAPTER 55
PROUD PARENT

In 1942 on June 22nd, at the age of nineteen, my son John joined the Royal Air Force Volunteer Reserve. Alice and I were very proud of him. He went away to be trained as a navigator, in a Tiger Moth over the Solent. During this time he would write to us frequently while he was away, and in typical practical joker form, during his training he wound up his mother by telling her in a letter that they had not been issued any knives and forks and that he was having to use a comb and a cardboard bus ticket to eat his food. Alice was of course equally horrified and distraught by this news.

After his training was complete he was deployed to Africa. He served with the Royal Air Force until the end of the Second World War in 1945, when he was very glad to return home to my wife and I physically intact, but somewhat mentally traumatised, as, I suspect, the majority of the participants in the war were. He never really told us any details about his wartime experiences and we left him to process what he had seen and felt in his own time. He trained to be a primary school teacher after the war. This was not a career that suited him, however and he went on to retrain as an accountant, a career which suited him far better, since he had always been really good with figures.

Jack's son, John Cornelius Rogers, during the Second
World War.

CHAPTER 56

HITLER DELAYED OUR HOLIDAY

Before the start of the Second World War my wife and I were frequent visitors to one of our favourite places, Shanklin, on the Isle of Wight. We would go there for the day, leaving our Singer car in Southsea and taking a steamer ferry over to Ryde on the Isle of Wight. We loved to spend the day wandering around and sitting on the beach. We were very excited to hear that some friends of ours planned to move over there and, once they had got themselves settled, we happily accepted their invitation to come and stay with them for a week in 1939, hoping it would distract our minds from our growing worries caused by the actions of Adolf Hitler.

The very morning we were due to set off, our plans were scuppered by a radio announcement telling us war had been declared. For mainland Great Britain, this news didn't have an immediate effect, but for the Isle of Wight it was a different story. The island was closer to France, where the German army was gathering, and the whole way of life over there was dramatically changed immediately. Firstly, all communications with the island were halted and all the tourists were evacuated to safety immediately. Then the defence operation was put into action. We were kept informed by our friends of the developments and their letters became a compelling read for us as the island was turned into a mini-fortress. Barbed wire was being put everywhere and mines were placed all over the main beaches in case the Germans decided to invade. No one was allowed to venture anywhere near the beaches any more for their own safety.

Further into the war it seemed that a German invasion was less likely, and the Isle of Wight became the site of planning and preparations for the Allies who were going to be reposted over to Normandy in France. These preparations included building the PLUTO pipeline, which would carry fuel under the English Channel, to be used by the Allied Forces when they reached the French beaches. The massive telescopic pipeline was several feet in diameter and was pieced together on Shanklin beach. Then it was launched out into the English Channel. It really was a tremendous feat of engineering.

Our friends kept in touch with us throughout the war and, in 1945, when the hostilities finally came to an end, they remembered their invitation to us, six years previously. We were eager to leave London, where we had been stuck for the duration of the war, and visit them to see everything they had told us about with our own eyes. It was a very strange kind of holiday. The beach was still covered with barbed wire and we were unable to venture onto the beach because of the mines which had been placed there. I do remember that the food on that holiday was fantastic. The Isle of Wight didn't seem to have had the same shortages of food we had experienced during the war and they were not suffering from rationing. I ate so much that week that my trousers were too tight when we left! I always thought of the names on the Isle of Wight as being very curious. You have Cowes that cannot be milked, Needles you cannot thread and Newport and Freshwater you cannot drink!

PART VII
AFTER THE WAR

CHAPTER 57
A ROYAL WEDDING

In 1947 I bought my first TV set. The war was over and my son John was back safely, living with us once again, and between the three of us, we decided we would really like to own a television. It was a ten inch Pye model. We were one of the first families in the area to have a television set and pretty much half of the neighbourhood came over to our house on 20th November, 1947 to watch the royal wedding of Her Royal Highness Princess Elizabeth to Prince Philip, at Westminster Abbey. They had become engaged only four months before their wedding, which seemed like a bit of a hurry to me! It was amazing to be able to watch such an event from the comfort of your own living room. We all dressed up smartly in our Sunday best, as if we were attending the actual wedding and could be seen by the prince and princess themselves! Alice put on quite a spread of party food for everybody to enjoy after the broadcast and we decorated our living room as best we could. We couldn't believe how clear the picture was and that we were able to see the expressions on the faces of all the people at the wedding. At the time I had no idea I would later appear on the television myself on more than one occasion!

CHAPTER 58
RELOCATION TO SUSSEX

I had always enjoyed my day trips down to the south coast, particularly Brighton, from a very early age, and decided it would be pleasant and possibly more healthy, to escape the smogs of London and live near the sea, so we bought a little bungalow on Deal Avenue in a town called Seaford, more or less halfway between East-bourne and Brighton.

We had just settled in nicely in that town, when unfortunately my wife, Alice became very ill suddenly with a blood clot in her leg. Sadly there was nothing the doctors could do to help her and she passed away soon after from thrombosis, when the blood clot moved to her heart on 4th March 1959, not very long after our relocation. I was heartbroken. We had finally taken the plunge and moved away from London and had so many plans for what we would do with our new life by the seaside together, but unfortunately none of them were meant to be. My son was living in lodgings in London at the time and moved down from London to join me in Sussex to keep me company. It was a shock to lose her so suddenly after thirty eight years of marriage, and another tragic time in my life. Both John and I missed Alice terribly, but having each other around every day helped us both to get over her loss gradually.

JOHN BEGAN WORKING FOR THE EASTBOURNE COUNTY Council as an accountant and he met his future wife, a delightful Yorkshire woman named Elizabeth Mary Isle in Eastbourne, through mutual friends. They were married on October 10th, 1966 in Seaford, Sussex.

John's cousin Ted Ralph was supposed to be John's best man at the wedding, but unfortunately, the Ralph family experienced car trouble on their way to Seaford and developed a puncture near Chichester. They were then up against the clock to get to the church on time and only arrived as John and Elizabeth were leaving the church. Without mobile phones in those days there was no way for Ted to let us know what was happening, so when he didn't appear to be going to show up I stepped in as John's best man in the church in order to pass the wedding ring to John. I was relieved when Ted showed up before the reception, though, since he was the one who had written a speech, although, if necessary, I'm sure I could have regaled the wedding guests with a couple of monologues and a few songs!

John, Elizabeth and I moved to a larger semi-detached house in Seaford, on Vicarage Lane and, just under two years later on June 23rd, 1968, my only grandchild, Susan Louise Rogers was born. I doted on her and would often take her for walks to the local park and when she was old enough to go to playschool and then primary school, I would often walk to meet her at the gates and then the two of us would walk home together through the town, often stopping for an ice cream along the way. It was lovely to have them around, but in 1974 John accepted a job with the County Council in Lincoln, Lincolnshire and they decided to relocate there, while I became the lodger of a lady I knew from the Old Aged Pensioners' Club, Mrs Edna New.

CHAPTER 59
OLD AGE PENSIONERS CLUB

In the late 1960s and 1970s I was regional secretary of the National Federation of Old Age Pensioners' Clubs in Sussex. After my retirement from the shoe repair business, and following the death of my wife, this club became a beloved hobby and social lifeline for me. We would arrange a summer holiday coach trip each year for all the members of the club to enjoy. One particular year our destination was Scotland, as was often the case. We were traveling by coach, as usual, but unfortunately, this time we were given an older coach for our trip rather than the new one we usually had. One day we were on our way back from a day out in Glencoe, when suddenly there was a loud juddering noise coming from the coach's engine, followed by a jolt, and our coach broke down a few miles from Glencoe. We appeared to be in the middle of nowhere; all we could see around us were soaring heather-covered hillsides, trees and a narrow winding road. We decided to get out to investigate the vehicle and to our dismay it turned out that one of the axles had broken.

Now what on earth were we supposed to do? Someone

would have to walk and try and find a public telephone. There was a village about five miles away, so the driver set off on foot to see if he could find help there. That left around fifty of us wondering what we could do while we awaited his return and some form of rescue.

All of a sudden someone noticed some smoke coming from what appeared to be a small shed about a hundred yards away on the roadside. Since we had nothing else to do we decided to have a look at the little shack and see where the smoke was coming from. The building was deserted, but we knocked on the door and eventually a little old lady opened it up for us. What a surprise! We had somehow managed to discover a highland tea room right in the middle of nowhere, just when we needed one! How the lady proprietor made a living, I don't know, as only two cars had passed us by in the last hour and it appeared to be a fairly remote area.

We were spitting feathers by this time and in need of a cup of tea to boost our failing moods. All fifty of us crowded inside the tearoom. The poor lady was very startled by our unexpected visit! I doubt she had ever seen so many parched pensioners inside her premises all at once; she was more used to serving the odd long distance lorry. She managed to find enough cups and saucers and brought out some big kettles to make us some tea, as well. She tried to serve us all, but eventually there were just too many of us for her to cope with. In the end she told us where the tea was, where the cups were and the biscuits and basically just let us make our own refreshments! We formed a little production line and soon had things under control with some of us making tea, some of us drinking tea and some of us washing the cups and saucers afterwards. Since the arithmetic was a bit too much for the lady, we had a whip round and gave her a tidy sum of money as a thank you for saving us from dying of thirst! She was very pleased with her day's earnings!

A couple of hours later, just as it was getting dark, our driver returned, having been to Fort William and managed to commandeer a double decker bus for us. He had contacted the depot in Glasgow first, and had learned that all the buses were being used on the city's streets, since there had been a deluge in the area, which had flooded the underground railway system. So all the local buses were being used as emergency transport instead, since the trains were unable to run. We all gladly boarded the bus from Fort William and returned to our hotel, just in time for our evening meal!

⚜

ANOTHER TIME WE CHARTERED A COACH TO RHYL, North Wales for the OAP club's summer holiday, and during our stay we saw a poster for a talent contest. The contest was going to take place at the town hall and we decided to go along for a spot of entertainment. When we arrived, the organisers were trying to decide whether or not to cancel the show since only two acts had signed up. Our pensioners group was always putting on shows for our own entertainment, so we decided to help out and throw together an impromptu performance. We included several Gilbert and Sullivan songs, some Shakespearean mono- logues and a few jokey bits which all went down very well. To our delight and amazement we won first prize. Admit- tedly there weren't many other entrants and the £1 prize money didn't really go far between our large group!

Dᴜʀɪɴɢ ᴏᴜʀ ᴛɪᴍᴇ ɪɴ Rʜʏʟ ᴡᴇ ᴍᴀɴᴀɢᴇᴅ ᴛᴏ ʜᴀᴠᴇ another exciting escapade which gave new meaning to the phrase 'needing to spend a penny'. We were out for a day trip to Betws-y-Coed in Snowdonia, visiting the Swallow Falls waterfall and river, which has a lovely old garden and tea house. The toilets at this place were very nice, surrounded by hedges around seven feet tall and entered via a turnstile which required a penny being spent by placing it into a slot on the turnstile before you could enter and 'spend a penny'. After our visit to the lovely tea house, all fifty of us were in need of the facilities and we eagerly formed a queue behind the first lady, who dutifully dropped her penny into the slot in the turnstile. Somehow the penny got stuck and the turnstile would not budge when she pushed against it! We were horrified, fifty of us desperate to go to the loo and no way to get the penny unjammed from its slot.

We put our heads together and came up with a plan of action which was unconventional to say the least! A couple of us more athletic gentlemen clambered up on top of the turnstile, puffing and panting as we went. We were all pensioners, remember, and this took a fair amount of balance and energy! Another couple of chaps climbed up and over and positioned themselves on the ground inside the turnstile, in front of the door to the lavatories. Then we began the emergency mission. We formed a kind of 'conveyor belt' lifting up the ladies over the turnstile and setting them down safely on the other side. We would haul them up to the top, then turn them around to face the direction in which they were traveling and hand them down to the men at the bottom, who grabbed their legs and carefully saw them safely down to earth once more, so they could go about their business! It was tough going after a while and we had to work quickly to avoid anyone having an 'accident', but our labours and our system of 'lift, turn and catch' paid off and indeed saved us quite a few pennies!

CHAPTER 60
BURIED ALIVE - AGAIN!

As I mentioned earlier, my son, John and his young family had moved up north to Lincoln in 1974, and I had remained in Seaford, moving into Richmond Court as flatmate to Mrs. Edna New, the treasurer of the Old Age Pensioners' Club, who was a very dear friend of mine.

In 1987 I was still living in Richmond Court, and I was in the habit of listening to the news and weather on the BBC, before heading off to bed each evening. On this one particular evening, October 16th, I had listened to weatherman Michael Fish reassuring a lady that she needn't worry, as there was no hurricane on its way.

What followed is history - the worst storm I have ever experienced in my long life, and the worst storm witnessed on the south coast of England in nearly three centuries. It brought so much devastation in its wake, it was quite incredible. The radio broadcast warned of a severe storm and the dangers of being outside, but I was safely tucked up in bed and feeling quite cozy, so I wasn't really concerned. The wind was howling outside as I turned out my bedside light, but I didn't think too much of it. After a while, however, I became aware of the wind getting louder and more terrifying, and I wasn't able to get to sleep, so I put my head right under all of the covers to try and block out the noise of the wind and I think, again, Lady Luck was looking after me. Suddenly my window slammed open with a huge bang and shattered. There were shards of glass and wood splinters from the window frame all over my bed, but luckily I was protected by my bed covers being over my head! There were a lot of ornaments on a chest of drawers by my bed and they had also been flung onto the bed. Plaster was falling from the ceiling onto my head like rain! Half of the roof had been torn away and there was debris everywhere. I had to lift pieces of broken plaster away from me before I was able to get out of my bed. When I finally managed to get out of bed I could see that my wardrobe had been pushed just far enough in front of my door that I was unable to get out of the room. It was a very shocking and upsetting experience!

The torn curtains were fluttering in the wind, which by now had luckily died down somewhat. My friend and neighbour, Bunny Baxter came downstairs to see if I was all right but I had to tell him I was trapped in my room by the wardrobe. After I emptied the wardrobe, and with a lot of pushing and shoving I was able to escape from the bedroom to find a similar sight in the living room! It was such an unexpected shock, the rooms were totally destroyed! It seemed Richmond Court, being quite close to the seafront, had been hit pretty badly. The roof was damaged and some nearby garages had had their roofs ripped off completely. All along the seafront in Seaford was the same - whole trees had been torn out of the ground and left strewn about the place like firewood. It was terrifying to see. The local council came round to the flat to inspect the damage and decide what, if anything, could be done to rectify things, but there was so much destruction it was quite impossible for them to repair everything. They boarded up all of the broken windows as a temporary solution, but the place was looking pretty forlorn.

My son, John came down to Sussex straightaway to see how bad things were. He was very shocked by the sight that met him and immediately decided I would need to pack up all of my belongings and go to live with him, Elizabeth and Susan once again, this time in Lincoln. I had been to stay with them many times since they moved from Sussex and had got to know Lincoln a little and really liked it there, so it didn't feel like I would be moving somewhere completely unknown, which was reassuring. I was sad to leave Sussex after so many years living there, I was 93 by then and somewhat set in my ways. However, I was excited to be staying with my family again, while John tried to find a more suitable apartment for me in a 'sheltered accommodation' set-up, with meals provided and a warden on site in case I needed any help. Rasen House fit the bill and an apartment became available before too long. I was one of ten residents at Rasen House and for most of my time there, I was the only man. I did love referring to the other residents as my harem and entertaining them with my old songs and stories. As you will see, the move to Lincoln was also to bring a slice of unexpected fame my way!

CHAPTER 61
REACHING A CENTURY

On 21st March, 1994, I celebrated my one hundredth birthday. I was, by then, living at Rasen House, in Lincoln, and they put on quite a party for me with a lovely cake and many cards and presents. A large number of my friends and family members were in attendance and of course it gave me an opportunity to put on a little show, entertaining my fellow residents with a few jokes and monologues. They seemed to enjoy themselves and I certainly did. I never pass up an opportunity to do a little spot of entertaining! On reaching the grand old age of 100, I received a telegram from Queen Elizabeth II. It stated:

I AM DELIGHTED TO SEND YOU MY WARM CONGRATULATIONS ON YOUR ONE HUNDREDTH BIRTHDAY, TOGETHER WITH MY BEST WISHES FOR AN ENJOYABLE CELEBRATION.

ELIZABETH R.

Of course I had already received a letter from her grandfather, King George V back in 1918, so I was proud to yet again receive correspondence from royalty. Little did I know I would be hearing from her with telegrams again on the occasion of my 105th and 106th birthdays! My great-nephew, Christopher Ralph, son of Ted Ralph, my son's cousin, wrote me a poem with the help of his family:

Uncle Jack's Special Day

In Lincoln City
On the first day of spring,
From miles around
The people did bring
Portraits and coins
And unusual things,
All to the Antiques Roadshow.

❦

The public impatiently
Stood in a queue,
Awaiting Hugh Scully
And the rest of the crew.
Then the camera rolled;
The clock struck two,
And they opened the Antiques Roadshow.

❦

There were platters of silver
And old Persian rugs.
There were musical boxes,
And bedpans, and jugs.
There were tables, and hat-stands
All riddled with bugs.
There were bottles, and moth-eaten bureaus.

There were cuckoo-clocks, cellos,
And dolls by the score.
There were fine china ornaments,
And teapots galore.
There were even stuffed tigers
From Bangalore
On display at the Antiques Roadshow.

The experts had scrutinised
Everything there,
Had displayed splendid knowledge,
And valued with care,
'Til at last one exhibit,
An old wooden chair,
Still remained at the Antiques Roadshow.

The owner, a man
Of some local renown,
Was invited on camera.

He sat himself down
On the chair, while the experts
Began to expound
Upon what a rare sample was found here.

❧

"Just look at those legs...
So well-grained, not a crack;
And the seat is so firm,
With a perfect straight back.
It's a wonderful piece!
Must be worth quite a stack,
It's really the best thing around here!"

❧

"It's not local" said one
With a knowing sniff,
"Made in London I'd say,
There's a slight smokey whiff.
My guess would be
King Street, 'Ammersmiff,
Circa 1930."

❧

"I'd agree," said another,
"But I'll be still more bold.
It's Victorian
If truth be told.
There's a date on one arm.
It's a hundred years old.

And look! It's not even dirty!"

❦

"Wait a bit" said the man,
('Twas Jack Rogers, you've guessed),
"Do you mean that this chair
Excels all the rest?"
"No. The chair's fit for firewood.
We mean you. You're the best...
The best of a great generation."

❦

Uncle Jack, we are thankful
You've always been there
With a joke and a card-trick,
And a heart that cares...
And so we are grateful
For all that you are...
The best of a great generation.

PART VIII
FAME AT LAST!

CHAPTER 62

THE WORLD'S OLDEST
NEWSPAPER COLUMNIST

When I reached the grand old age of 103, in 1997, I was approached by Jason Mellor, a young journalist from the local newspaper, The Lincolnshire Echo. He had heard that there was an elderly gentleman living in Rasen House with a lot of stories to tell and he wanted to hear my stories and would come and interview me each week, listen to my anecdotes, most of which I have retold here, and then write a column in the newspaper, which they decided to call 'The World's Oldest Columnist'.

The first column appeared in the newspaper on April 24th, 1997. The column became very popular locally and I was invited onto a few different TV programmes to be interviewed, including ITV's Central News, BBC's Look North and East Midlands Today, and there was some national interest. I became a local celebrity and received a lot of fan mail. In fact, one teacher set an assignment for her class to each write me a letter, or draw a picture of me, after having me into their school to talk to them about some of my experiences. It was lovely to receive all their pictures and letters and I thoroughly enjoyed meeting all of the teachers and children.

ON MY 104TH BIRTHDAY, MARCH 21ST 1998, MY colleagues at the Echo helped to arrange a very special birthday celebration for me. There were thirty guests, including civic dignitaries such as the Mayor of Lincoln, family, friends and an extra special surprise visit from some of the past members of my old regiment - the Sherwood Foresters, who came over from Newark to visit me, looking resplendent in their medals. They even brought along Corporal Derby, the ram who acts as their regimental mascot. Then we had a performance by the Lincolnshire Cadet Force Band, wearing their bright red uniforms and playing a number of songs including 'The Lincolnshire Poacher'. It brought a tear to my eye, I can tell you, as that was the tune we used to march to during the First World War. They had us going at 140 beats per minute which was extremely hard work, especially when you are fully kitted out! I was speechless with gratitude for everyone's efforts at organising such a fantastic party. It was probably the first time in my life I have ever been speechless! All of this happened outside in the courtyard at my home at Rasen House, Lincoln and the sun shone on us the whole time. An amazing singer called Dee Dee Lee came along and sang all the old wartime songs for us as well. Of course, when they asked me to oblige them with a few jokes and monologues I was eager to comply and thoroughly enjoyed myself! There was an enormous amount of food to be had as well, which is a good thing considering the large number of guests! We had a buffet in the morning and then after the entertainment a fantastic lunch was laid on, followed by a wonderful tea in the late afternoon. By the end of the day I was very full and pretty tired, but it had been a truly marvellous celebration.

❧

AT ONE POINT IN 1998, THE LINCOLN CITY COUNCIL came up with an innovative solution to get around the problem of getting from the town centre of Lincoln up the infamous Steep Hill to the historic part of the town at the top, where the cathedral and Norman-era castle are situated, among other, older, historic Roman remains. The idea was that they would use some electric powered vehicles, similar to the now defunct, old-fashioned milk floats belonging to Lincoln Co-Operative Society, to ferry people up and down the hill in a more eco-friendly manner. Steep Hill is considered a deterrent for many able-bodied people from reaching the historic areas of Lincoln and is an impossibility for the elderly and infirm.

The Echo asked me if I would like to go along and test out this method of travel and of course, I was only too happy to have another adventure, and then use my journalistic skills to report my findings to the newspaper. I thought it was a fantastic way to travel. The top speed was 20mph, about the same as my first old car which I bought in 1912. It was a very leisurely way to visit some of the city's harder to reach attractions. The new vehicles could seat up to twelve people and they could accommodate one wheelchair and were going to be free of charge. I thoroughly enjoyed my trip. It's a real shame the idea didn't take off, unfortunately, and residents were left with the more usual bus journeys to get up the Hill.

I WROTE SEVENTY-FIVE ARTICLES FOR THE Lincolnshire Echo with Jason's help, before deciding to retire at the grand old age of 104. I suppose the secret of my success in that endeavour has been the amazingly clear memory that I have been blessed with.

CHAPTER 63

CHEVALIER DE LA LÉGION D'HONNEUR

In October 1988, I received a letter from the French Embassy informing me that I had been chosen to be awarded the prestigious 'Chevalier de la Légion d'Honneur' medal from the French government, after they decided to extend this honour to all the Allied nations. They decided that two hundred of us remaining British veterans should receive the medal as a way of honouring those of us who fought bravely during the First World War, eighty years previously. The medal was presented to me in a moving ceremony at Rasen House, on December 15th 1998, by Bridget Cracroft Eley, Lord Lieutenant of Lincolnshire. Also present was Brigadier Tony Plummer, the county president of the Royal British Legion, the Mayor of Lincoln, Councillor Bud Robinson, as well as some members of my old regiment, the Sherwood Foresters and, of course, family members and friends. We had a moment of silence to remember all of those who had fallen in the conflict and I said the following words: "I am extremely grateful for two reasons. One, that I have been allowed to live this long to receive this, and secondly I am sure that it was meant, not only for me, but on behalf of the thousands and thousands that made the great sacrifice in the First World War." I was very moved and those words were heartfelt. A tear or two of reminiscence were shed that day, I can tell you!

CHAPTER 64
MORE BIRTHDAY TELEGRAMS
FROM THE QUEEN

My 105th birthday was also an occasion to remember. Once again I was visited by the remaining Sherwood Foresters and received another royal telegram from Queen Elizabeth II, which stated:

I WAS PLEASED TO HEAR THAT YOU ARE TO CELEBRATE YOUR ONE HUNDRED AND FIFTH BIRTHDAY ON SUNDAY 21ST MARCH. MY BEST WISHES TO YOU ON THIS WONDERFUL ACHIEVEMENT.

ELIZABETH R.

Rasen House put on yet another fantastic party for me with The City of Lincoln Band performing, and a bugle and drum band came over from Newark. The bugle and drum band was part of my old army unit, The Robin Hood Rifles Regiment of the Sherwood Foresters, and was composed of Bugle Major Owen Wheeldon, Band Sgt.

Peter Roebuck and Warrant Officer Bill Lawson. They performed very well. Brigadier Tony Plummer and the Mayor of Lincoln, Bud Robinson, and City Sheriff, Trevor Rook, also came along to wish me a happy birthday. I told them some of my wartime stories and anecdotes to keep them all entertained. At the end of the party The City of Lincoln Band played 'For He's a Jolly Good Fellow'. All in all it was another thoroughly enjoyable celebration.

My 106th birthday, in the year 2000, was also celebrated in style with yet another telegram from the Queen - that's three times she's written to me now, I think she may have a crush on me! This time it was more of a card than a telegram with a photo of herself on the front and inside it said:

IT GIVES ME GREAT PLEASURE TO SEND YOU MY SINCERE CONGRATULATIONS AND BEST WISHES ON THE OCCASION OF YOUR ONE HUNDRED AND SIXTH BIRTHDAY ON 21ST MARCH 2000.

ELIZABETH R.

It's hard to believe I have been alive in the 1800s, 1900s and now the 2000s! We had a smaller party at Rasen House this time, with friends and family in attendance. I had been asked what I would like to eat and I eagerly chose my favourite meal, roast lamb with plenty of mint sauce. I had been in hospital for a while following a fall just before Christmas, so it was lovely to be able to come out of hospital for the day of my party and see everyone at Rasen House again, having lived there for over a decade. At one point I was the only man living there, with ten elderly ladies. Of course I made it my priority at the time to keep them all entertained. I looked through all of my old photos while I was at Rasen House that day and had quite a time reminiscing over my long life. I was told I was Britain's oldest man and was certainly the oldest survivor of the First World War at that point in time. I had also been drawing an old age pension for more years than I had worked. What an amazing and in parts, bittersweet, life I have had!

❦

JACK ROGERS SADLY PASSED AWAY ON 13TH APRIL 2000, three weeks after his 106th birthday party, and is greatly missed by everyone who was lucky enough to know him.

TIMELINE

1894 Jack Rogers is born on March 21st.

1897 Jack is three - Queen Victoria's Diamond Jubilee.

1863 London Underground opened its first line between Paddington and Farringdon. It is the first underground railway in the world.

30th July 1900 Jack is six - London Underground Railway Line from Shepherds Bush to Bank is opened to the public and Jack and his father ride the rails.

1901 Jack is seven- End of the Boer War. Queen Victoria dies and King Edward VII is crowned.

1904 Jack is ten - Wilbur and Orville Wright make their first powered flight.

1908 Jack is fourteen - Henry Ford's Model T - the first mass-produced car - rolls off the production line.

1911 King George V is crowned.

1914 Jack is twenty - The First World War breaks out.

July 26th 1914 Jack's sister May marries her first husband, Will Price.

1915 Jack is twenty-one and enlists. He is then sent to France.

Easter 1916 Jack is sent over to help quell the Easter Rising in Dublin, Ireland.

July 1st 1916 - Nov 18 1916 - Battle of the Somme, along the River Somme in France.

July 31 1917 - Nov 6 1917: The Third Battle of Ypres, also known as the Battle of Passchendaele in Belgium. Jack is involved in this battle at the age of twenty-three.

1918 Jack is twenty-four and is taken prisoner by the Germans on his birthday (21st March). December signifies the end of The First World War.

March 29th 1920 Jack's friend and brother-in-law, Will Price dies in India

November 23rd 1920 Jack's sister May marries her second husband, Jim Hicks.

1921 Jack is twenty-seven and marries Alice Ralph.

August 22nd 1922 - Jim Hicks dies.

September 16th 1923 - Jack's sister Beat marries Fred Sutton.

1923 Jack is twenty-nine - Jack and Alice's son, John Cornelius Rogers is born on **December 17th**, named after Alice's brother Con (Cornelius).

December 14th 1924 - Jack's sister Rose marries Will Smith.

1927 Jack is thirty-three - the first 'talkie' film, 'The Jazz Singer' premieres.

March 17th 1928 - Jack's sister May marries her third husband, Alf Coombes.

June 4th 1933 - Jack's sister Minnie marries Alf Chapman.

June 21st 1933 - Jack's brother Freddie dies.

September 15th 1935 - Jack's sister Florrie marries Don Baird.

1936 Jack is forty-two - Jarrow Marchers walk to London.

May 17th 1938 - Jack's mother, Clara Rogers dies.

1939 Jack is forty-five - World War II breaks out and Jack becomes an ARP warden.

November 17th 1939 - Jack's father, Harry Rogers dies.

1940 Jack is forty-six - Makeshift navy evacuates the British Army from Dunkirk.

1945 Jack is fifty-one - Bomb is dropped on Hiroshima - end of World War II.

1953 Jack is fifty-nine - Queen Elizabeth II is crowned - Jack and neighbours watch it on TV.

1961 Jack is sixty-seven - Russians win the human space race when Cosmonaut Yuri Gagarin becomes the first human in space.

1968 Jack is seventy-four - his granddaughter, Susan Louise Rogers is born on June 23rd.

July 20, 1969 Jack is seventy-five - Apollo 11 lands on the moon.

1987 Jack is ninety-three - Hurricane on the South Coast of England - is reported as nothing to worry about by Michael Fish. Jack moves up to Lincoln.

1997 Jack is 103 and becomes the World's Oldest Columnist, writing a weekly column for the Lincolnshire Echo with the help of journalist Jason Mellor.

2000 Jack passes away on April 13th at the grand age of 106.

ABOUT THE AUTHOR

Sue Bavey is an English Mum of two, living in Massachusetts since 2003 with her husband, kids, a cat named Midnight, a bunny named Nutmeg, and a leopard gecko named Ziggy Stardust. This book is her grandfather, Henry John Rogers' biography.

Email: sue.bavey@gmail.com (Emails welcome).
Twitter: @SueBavey
Blog: My blog is at www.suelbavey.wordpress.com where I mostly write reviews of other people's books

Photos to accompany this book can be viewed at https://suelbavey.wordpress.com/lucky-jack-photo-gallery/

ACKNOWLEDGMENTS

I would like to thank both my mother, Elizabeth Rogers, for providing me with much of the source material for this book and Christopher Ralph, the family historian, who was able to provide a lot of photographs and historical information regarding both the Ralph and the Rogers families.

In addition to the material gathered during conversations with Jack and his sisters by the aforementioned family members, I have used the following sources, written by those who interviewed my grandfather during his long life:

- 'Veterans', by Richard van Emden (ISBN-10: 085052640X)
- 'Prisoners of the Kaiser', by Richard van Emden (ISBN-10: 1848840780)
- 'Once Upon a Wartime I', by Molly Burkett (ISBN-10: 0948204362)
- The original articles dictated by Jack Rogers to Jason Mellor for local English newspaper, The

Lincolnshire Echo, which I have reworded for
the purposes of this book.

I was lucky enough to find a wonderful editor in Alison
Williams - find her at https://alisonwilliamswriting.
wordpress.com/

I found some fabulous beta readers through the 'We Love
Memoirs' Facebook group. Thank you so much to Susan
Jackson, Debbie Johnson, Rebecca Hislop, Pat Ellis and
Mary Hollendoner for your useful suggestions and encour-
agement. We Love Memoirs is the friendliest group on
Facebook:
https://www.facebook.com/groups/welovememoirs

Rod Cox proofread the final draft and did a fantastic job.

I would like to thank my daughter, Ellie Bavey for her
inspired help with the cover design for this book.

Bjørn Larssen (josephtailor) did a fantastic job of format-
ting the manuscript and preparing it for publication
for me.

My friends (both on social media and in real life) who
agreed to read earlier drafts and encouraged me to
continue also deserve acknowledgement, especially author
friends Annie Buckley, Carl Rackman and Dan Fitzgerald.
Thank you all so much for your time and support.

I would also like to thank the Facebook group 'We Love
Memoirs' for sending me a joining gift entitled 'How to

Write a Bestselling Memoir' by Victoria Twead which came at a very helpful time!

Last but by no means least, I would of course also like to acknowledge the patience and support of my husband and children during this project. I appreciate their listening to certain stories, while I tried to decide what was funny or interesting enough to be included.

Printed in Great Britain
by Amazon